T0137552

Don't be Afraid Little Sister

Juddie Cline-Lindley

Order this book online at www.trafford.com
or email orders@trafford.com

Most Trafford titles are also available at major online book retailers.

© Copyright 2013 Juddie Cline-Lindley.
All rights reserved. No part of this publication may be reproduced, stored in a retrieval
system, or transmitted, in any form or by any means, electronic, mechanical, photocopying,
recording, or otherwise, without the written prior permission of the author.

Printed in the United States of America.

ISBN: 978-1-4269-1942-8 (sc)
ISBN: 978-1-4269-1943-5 (hc)

Library of Congress Control Number: 2009912985

Trafford rev. 07/18/2013

 www.trafford.com

North America & international
toll-free: 1 888 232 4444 (USA & Canada)
fax: 812 355 4082

Table of Contents

The following is a true story. Some of the names have been changed to protect the identity and respect the privacy of the characters portrayed.

PROLOGUE

The true story you are about to read is one of victory and triumph.

As a young Anglo woman running in fear of my safety and that of my two young children, I was somehow guided to the Navajo Reservation. It was there in a windswept, desolate location, that I learned the true love of a people. Two cultures crossed and became as one, through teachings of the Navajo who believe in dreams and occurrences where many Anglos care not to tread. The Navajo Reservation became my sanctuary and remains so to this day.

It has been said that I am a woman of many facets. One is a tender loving side to children and the elderly. Another is that of a cop, fiercely independent, a survivor willing to do the job. Yet another is when I suddenly break into short, matter of fact sentences, saying little but letting my words carry the impact, much like the Navajo who protected me.

Several prominent people in this book have passed on, but shall never be forgotten, their love deeply rooted in my heart and soul. Kee Benally, who afforded us protection and believed we were guided to the reservation. Albert Juan, because his actions and love of his savior destined Lake Valley to be my home. Benny Singer, my adoptive father and Navajo Medicine Man. PK Williams, who painted the picture for this book cover and Alice Becenti, friend and sister, whose courage was an inspiration to all that knew her.

Among the living there is Suzie Juan, whose love and prayers sustained me, her selfless actions keeping me alive. Patsy Singer, beloved wife of my adoptive father. Aunt Eleanor, Mary Lou, Charley and Marie Singer, Ben and Dee Mitchell, and my extended Navajo family.

This story is a "thank you," to the Navajo people and is long overdue. Words can never express the kindness and kindred spirit I feel when I am with my family, the Navajo. The warmth that welcomes me like a Pendleton blanket when I retreat to the Rez to renew my inner spirit, the smiles and laughter I share with family, the fry bread and ceremonies; children running, horses and sheep. The Rez is home to me.

MAY WE WALK IN BEAUTY

CHAPTER 1

Rhythms of the Reservation

The hot, bright sun streams through the hogan windows waking me from a sound sleep. In the distance I hear the faint cry of sheep and a barking dog trained to herd them. Their owner will be close by. I wipe sand from my eyes and brush my hand gently across my face. The blowing sand through the night has seeped through the cracks. It spreads across the room as though sprinkled by a fairy's wand.

"Gently does it Jude," I remind myself. The sand embeds my sunburned face, causing me to grimace at the slightest touch. I will ask Kee to bring medicine from the trees to rub on my face. Then I will hide from view for a time because my face will turn a deep, shiny, Navajo red. When the kids see it they will howl with laughter as they have always done before. I am embarrassed by the sunburn itself and would cover my face with a towel or pillow slip and hide from humanity if only it were not so sore.

My throat is so dry, that it's difficult to swallow. Time to get up and take a drink of spring water from the open can. I fill my cup and slowly sip the water, savoring every drop. The dryness in my throat eases. Now I am ready for that second cup. I glance up at the small hand mirror someone has attached to the wall. I look awful. My hair stands out like a cartoon of someone whose finger is stuck in a wall socket. My face is burnt a crimson red, contrasting starkly with my blue eyes.

I shake the sand from the sheet and blanket that has gathered during the night. After breakfast I will sweep the floor, and repeat it several times throughout the day.

I'll let the kids sleep in. That way I'll have my privacy and I can take a sponge bath from the wash basin. Anything is better than the nasty-smelling community showers. The water smells of oil and leaves thick "gunk" in my hair. I'll gather fresh clothes for the kids and drive to the hot springs in Bisti so they can bathe. I'll wash my hair while I'm there.

A bath and a wet brush run through my tangled hair refreshes me. I brush my teeth and pull on a long, homemade Navajo skirt. I choose to wear a long-sleeved velvet blouse instead of my cotton shirt even though it's going to be another excruciating, hot day. I'll sweat profusely, but this is Navajo attire and one must obey the "protocol." Besides, this clothing was made for me by the Navajo women. They wear it daily, and I shall, too.

It's time to wake the kids and feed them breakfast of fried eggs and bread.

"Come on guys! Wake up sleepy heads! We don't want to waste all this beautiful sun!"

Moans and groans follow. Slowly, they wake and rub sand from their eyes.

"Ouch!" John cries out, "that hurts!"

I know the sand stings his eyes and I quickly bring him a wash cloth dipped in water. He wipes, and then smiles his thanks.

Hearing the sound of John's voice, the coyote puppy runs to him licking his face. There is little protest. Laughter follows as John hugs the ugly creature Kee Benally gave him. Seeing the smile on my son's face warms me like hot chocolate on a cold winter day. For the first time in my life I feel peace. I am free from the torment and heartbreak of my childhood.

I wish only the best for my children. I want to hear them laugh and listen quietly as they experience life. I will be there for them, waiting in the shadows if need be for the rest of their lives. I will always love them; not smother them. I think of their education and material needs. And I worry. I say a silent prayer asking for God's help. "You're all I have, Lord. Please help me raise my children." I sigh and feel better. God won't let me down, I reassure myself.

The kids trail outside to use the bathroom with the coyote puppy yipping at their feet. Once again I warn them to kick the old wood planks before sitting down, just in case a rattlesnake has crawled inside. I am always wary for their safety. There are so many hazards and medical help is far away.

I fry their eggs on an old stove hooked up to a propane tank. I watch the kids through the cracked window pane. There are no curtains. The sun streaks through the dark walls of the hogan. Soon it warms with laughter as the kids come inside. I call out to them to wash their hands in the basin. There are more giggles as the puppy nips at their heels, then jumps to lick their hands. Losing his balance, he tumbles over. I smile. Kee knew what was best for my son. He brought laughter and joy when he gave John that ugly creature. I have no regrets.

"Hurry and eat kids," I call out, "We're going to Bisti to the hot springs. Kee will be here this afternoon so we have to hurry."

John asks to take the coyote. I protest slightly then grab an old fruit jar from the cupboard and fill it with water for him. Both kids smile and scramble into the old car putting the "creature" between them. Quickly I rinse out two more jars and fill them with spring water using the dipper. I clutch them to my chest as I carry the towels and a bar of soap to the car, as well.

I listen to the kids' incessant chatter all the way to Bisti and back. The sun is hot and the kids are tired as we arrive back at the hogan. The coyote survived the trip without a problem. As soon as the car door opens the pup leaps out and pees on a dried tumbleweed. The kids "single file it" to the outside toilet as well, waiting their turn.

A quick lunch of fried Spam sandwiches follow. Cool water to drink and appreciative smiles cause me to pause and think that life could get no better. We are happy.

Soon a dust ball rises in the wind, tumbling high in the sky.

"Kee's coming!" John shouts.

He's right. Kee emerges from his rickety old truck with squeaky brakes. A broad smile crosses his face as he sees John standing at the open hogan door to greet him.

"Ya ta hey, John," Kee calls out as he lights from the truck and shakes John's little hand. "How's your ornery coyote do' in?" The smile does not leave his face.

Kee is proud of John. Or maybe Kee is proud of himself. John is a "man child" but he is also a good pupil and eager to learn Navajo way. Kee teaches John like he is his grandson. He never raises his voice and is always patient. Sometimes he puts his head back in laughter at some of John's questions. "That John sure is funny," he'll occasionally chuckle.

I fry Kee a Spam sandwich and give him a cup of spring water.

"Thank you sis," is his only response as he quickly consumes it.

Kee pulls an old chair to the center of the room.

"John, come here," he calls out, "it's time for your lesson."

John quickly gathers at his feet and I stand a short distance away, listening as Julie plays with a rag doll nearby.

"Today's lesson is on witchers; the evil one." Kee speaks in hushed tones. He is uncomfortable talking about this subject, yet he feels it is needed. This is not the time to ask questions. It is the time to listen. There is a purpose for this talk. Time will tell.

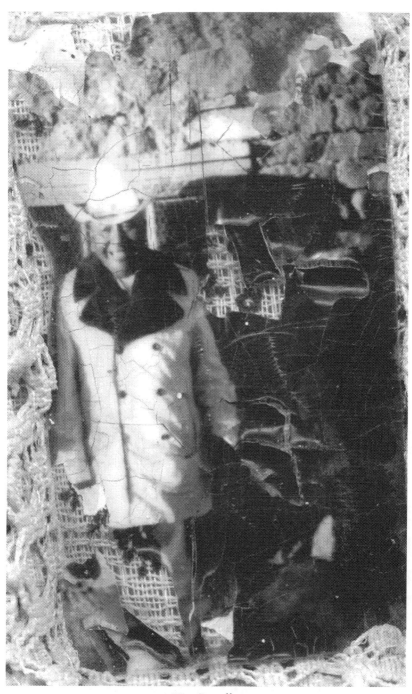

Kee Benally

I listen somewhat fearful. I resolve to myself that if "the witcher" ever comes after me or my children, I will fight back. I will not let him win. Kee glances my way and sees the determination on my face. My teeth are clinched. My jaw tightens. He looks pleased. He knows I will fight back.

The lesson is over, still leaving me with a lot of unanswered questions and a feeling of uneasiness. I will watch the children even closer.

As Kee climbs in his truck he calls out that there's a meeting tonight and he'll be by to pick us up at Navajo time. I smile, knowing that means "when the sheep are gathered." We wave goodbye as the dust bowl follows him down the dirt lane. I sigh. "How many white women have lived on the reservation and experienced this type of friendship with Native Americans?" I ask myself. The privilege is mine to savor.

I put the kids down for a nap knowing it may be a long night. Once they fall asleep I stand near the bedside. Just watching them. Ever so thankful they are mine. The innocence from a child's face should never be erased.

Lately, I've had an uneasy feeling. Almost like I am being watched. I've seen no one. But it was just a *feeling*. I say nothing to Kee. I have no proof. No tangible evidence. I do not want to loose my credibility by speaking too soon and sounding afraid to this mystical people.

Questions enter my mind. Why did Kee choose today's lesson on witchers? What is his purpose? He seems uneasy talking about it. Why? Are the witchers so evil, they should be feared?

The sound of the coyote yipping jars me from my thoughts. A fancy red truck is coming down the road. I recognize it as belonging to the "Bisti Boy's" folks. I step outside smiling.

They are both very large Navajo. A seemingly compatible couple. It is clear they like fry bread and mutton stew. The woman gazes downward when greeting me. Almost as though she is embarrassed or shy. Yet the warmth in her voice tells me she likes me. She is dressed in traditional attire; long flowing skirt and hair pulled back in the traditional Navajo bun. Her husband is gregarious and robust. He smiles and shakes my hand warmly. Still his eyes never quite meet mine. I invite them in for a drink of water. With heads somewhat lowered, they quickly exchange glances at one another. They seem surprised at my invitation. The husband nods his approval and they enter the hogan. A Navajo's hogan is his private area. Many times relatives are met outside and are not invited to enter. It will take time. But they will learn. This strange white woman has a few customs of her own.

I give them a drink of water, talking all the while. There is a purpose for my chatter. I want to make them feel comfortable and welcome.

The kids are beginning to stir. The coyote hears the yawns and quickly lopes to them with tail wagging and slobbering tongue protruding from his mouth. The Navajo laugh.

Kee brought me a pound of hamburger in an old ice chest yesterday. He picked up some ice at the trading post, as well. It is melted now but the meat is still cold. This will be an early dinner and I will invite my friends to stay. They accept, still looking puzzled. I am amused by this.

"Just wait until they eat my spaghetti," I chuckle to myself.

My incessant chattering succeeds. They are comfortable and talking back. The man speaks good English. The woman's is broken. Still we are able to communicate and learn from one another.

The woman wants to teach me how to do Julie's hair back in the Navajo bun. I eagerly accept while her husband watches approvingly.

Upon leaving they each shake my hand. The woman presses an object into my hand. I quickly look and smile. It is a beautiful ring. I question them about the stone and the origin. The woman says her husband is a silversmith, and he made it. As I thank them, the woman lowers her head and gives out a nervous giggle. The man looks me squarely in the eyes for the first time. I see pride on his face.

Navajo way is to give "love gifts." My new friends bestowed this lovely gift on me. I feel humble. I also feel undeserving.

They leave but the feeling of warmth remains in me. I will wear my new gift to the meeting tonight.

I get a wet cloth and quickly wash the kids' hands and faces, removing all traces of the spaghetti meal.

"Kee will be here shortly. Hurry John, comb your hair. Julie, put your shoes back on." I repeat myself half a dozen times. Kee is patient, but when he is ready, he doesn't like to wait.

The sun starts to go down and I hear the clang of Kee's old truck coming down the road. I am waiting outside with the kid's in tow when he pulls up. The coyote is outside and the door shut securely behind me. There is no lock.

I hoist the kids up into the truck while Kee remains behind the wheel smiling.

"It should be a good meeting tonight, sis. Brownwater's going to preach. He's the one I've been telling you about."

"Oh Good, Kee. Does he preach in Navajo or English? Not that I care."

Kee grunts his approval.

The meeting place is an old converted crudely built "sheep shed". The Navajo house the animals in them from the winter storms. In the hot summers they are converted into meeting places or spare housing for relatives.

The small room is already packed and old folding chairs, both metal and wooden are crammed next to each other. Kee secures us seating, and as usual, retreats to the doorway to greet friends.

The heat is stifling. Mixed with the close contact of others, it is hard for the kids to sit still and they begin to squirm in their seats. A woman throws her Pendleton blanket across the chair next to me. The wool fringe hits me in the face, stinging my eye. It is an accident and I ignore any discomfort.

The preacher works his way forward on the dirt-impacted floor. The Navajo listen intently. Some look skeptical while others look pleased and seem to believe what he says about this man, named Jesus.

It is a long meeting and people are beginning to leave. Soon the sound of many truck engines starting drowns out the preacher's voice. He realizes he has gone on too long. He quickly offers a closing prayer. The meeting is over.

The kids squirmed throughout, but were pretty patient. Now, they can stretch their legs. In a moment's notice they find little friends to play with near the doorway. I caution them to stay inside until I find Kee. He is nearby visiting with friends, as usual.

"This man seems to know everyone," I muse to myself.

Kee looks up and sees me. He knows it is time to go. He tells his friends goodbye, and tells me to "round" the kids up and he'll meet us at the truck.

In short order, the kids pile into the truck. They are already yawning and will be fast asleep. I keep them awake by talking to them until we reach the hogan.

The same uneasy feeling begins sweeping over me as I get the kids inside, using the headlights on Kee's truck for visibility. I light the kerosene lantern and wave goodbye.

I dress the kids for bed and have them stand back as I shake the sand from their blanket. I hold the lantern closer to inspect the sheet, brushing my hand across it. The kids are tired and will have restful sleep tonight, I say to myself. I help them say their prayers in Navajo, kissing them both on the head when they are finished. The last thing I say to them every night is, "I love you." This night is no exception.

I walk to my bed and set the lantern down on a small crude stand. Suddenly, I think I see something scurrying under the blanket. I grab the blanket with one hand and whisk it off the bed. Shaking it furiously, I am determined to destroy "the intruder." A large scorpion drops off and with tail up, seems to want a "stand off." *I win.*

Before dressing for bed, I want to look at the full moon "just one more time." I stand at the open hogan door letting the cool night air flitter down my arms and gently caress my face. The breeze is chilly but inviting. The sky seems low and touchable. Somehow, I feel warm inside. I am lucky. I am blessed. The peace I feel right now, at this very moment, is priceless. Finally, I have a family that loves me. I have found acceptance. I have been given a people that feel no compelling need to change me, or the person I am.

I have been given a new life. A new beginning for my children.

"Dear God, please let this feeling last forever."

The scorpions, rattlesnakes and now this "witcher" Kee talked about today cannot take this euphoria away from me. Somehow, I feel assured that this feeling, and these people will never leave me. I am happy.

CHAPTER 2

Destiny: Life Before Navajo Land

The tranquil setting of a Midwest farm where people sit on porches sipping lemonade while speaking lovingly to each other would seem almost heavenly. It should because it's fiction.

I grew up on an Iowa farm with 13 brothers and sisters. There were always chores, starting early in the morning and lasting until dark. Regardless of gender, we were expected to work in the hay fields, milk the cows, and care for the livestock. Momma had a huge garden and insisted that I pull the weeds by hand, so in the summer that was added to my list of chores. Complaining would get me nowhere, so even when my back and legs ached badly, I kept my mouth shut or the sting of the willow switch across my body would be the answer. Momma always insisted I scrub the floors by hand, three times. First to soak the floor in hot, sudsy water. Then scrub it, and go over it a third time with clear water. That's the way she had to do it when growing up and was adamant, I could do the same. Dishwater had to have bleach in it for cleanliness, wrecking havoc on my hands.

Most of the older kids had left home by this time. It always seemed like there was too much work and too little care being passed around. Maybe I needed a little love and attention because even at a very young age I was ornery and rebellious. And I was not alone. My "partner" was my little brother, John.

The original farmhouse was a big old two story wood structure. When I was three the house caught fire with a trio of us little ones trapped upstairs in our cribs. Momma was working in the yard and saw the flames shooting through the roof. Braving the fire, she rescued all three of us. The house burnt to the ground and everything was lost with the exception of the clothes we wore. Other farm families pitched in with food and clothing, and provided us with a place to live until Daddy was able to rebuild. The new house was much smaller partly because he was adamant about not owing for things, and proved his point many times when somehow he managed to temporarily fix a piece of farm equipment over and over until he had saved enough to buy a new tractor or combine.

Daddy, a staunch Catholic, was slender and handsome with a charming personality and winning smile. I often heard women comment on his good looks and dark hair, as though it were wishful thinking on their part. Everyone loved him. Everyone except me. He was cold, unfeeling and unemotional. I do not remember him ever putting his arm around me, ever telling me he loved me, or ever giving me encouraging words of any kind. Instead he would rage that "I acted too much like my mother." Years later I realized he couldn't stand me because every time he looked my way, it was like looking in the mirror at himself.

I was a quick study though, and loved to learn from Daddy; whether he was talking to other farmers, or negotiating the price on farm equipment or livestock. I trailed after him just to listen and learn. I'm sure he didn't want me around, but as long as I stayed in the background, he tolerated my presence. When neighboring farmers came to the house to visit, I would sit on the floor in the corner out of the way and listen. I learned how to negotiate prices, and lots of curse words as a bonus. The next day I would go to school and repeat the new words for all the kids. That made me the center of attention if only for a few fleeting moments. Momma, however, was not amused when she heard about my new expertise. She grabbed a bar of soap and washed my mouth out as I gagged and spit.

One time in my life Daddy showed a concern for me that I almost mistook for love. I had terrible leg cramps with unbearable pain and didn't eat for several days. I remember lying in bed, moaning and crying. Daddy stood at the bedroom door and told me to get up and get dressed; he would take me to see Doc Cunningham. I said no. He didn't pressure me; simply walked away. Twelve of us had been born at home and going to the doctor was rare, so I was probably afraid of dying there.

Because money was scarce, the favorite home remedy was horse salve. Once I stepped on a rusty nail as I swung off the horse, embedding it so deeply in my bare foot that I had to use my other foot to press down the old board it was in so I could pry it out. I remember holding my bloody foot over water, slapping the horse salve on, while wiping tears away so the others wouldn't tease me about being a sissy.

To get on Daddy's "good side" the unwritten rule was to ask him about the cattle. He loved his cattle and even named some. (I don't think he could remember all of his children's names sometimes, but his cattle were special.) When I wanted to manipulate him I would trail after him pretending to be interested in his stupid cows. Once as a reward for my keen interest, he bought me a candy bar, which I devoured. Then I made a big mistake. I bragged to the other kids about my chocolate treat. After that it was, "Why did Juddie get a candy bar and I didn't?" Other voices chimed in. That was the end of my treats from Daddy. But the taste and smell of that luscious Peter Paul Mound's (or now the lack of it) taught me a valuable lesson. Keep your mouth shut!

We were all expected to ride horses. I'm not sure of Daddy's reasoning, but he started us off early. I remember him lifting me up and placing me on a horse one day. I was so little and scared. It felt like I was 50 feet in the air. Daddy stepped away leaving me there by myself, grabbing at the mane with my small hands. Suddenly, the horse reared and threw me onto the hard ground. I lay there, dirty, skinned and sobbing. Instead of wiping away my tears, Daddy loomed over me demanding that I shut up. "Get back up on that horse and show him whose boss!" Then he swooped me up and put me back on the horse.

Daddy's action, though cruel, taught me a lesson that I have carried with me for the rest of my life. When life gets me down and obstacles or circumstances seem insurmountable, I tell myself to "get back up on that horse and show him whose boss." It hasn't always been easy, but a stubbornness and determination was instilled in me that day. Some "tough" things have happened occasionally throughout my life, but I have steadfastly refused to accept defeat and choose to fight with an inner strength and toughness.

Momma had been forced to quit school in the 8th grade when her mother died, leaving her to help raise younger twin brothers, and other siblings. It must have been a tremendous burden for such a young girl, while her dad worked in the coal mines of Kentucky.

She married dad when she was in her teens, only able to guess about her true age. Like many others, she was born at home and couldn't find the family Bible where records of birth were written.

Dad's family never accepted her. After all, she was this little uneducated, non-Catholic hillbilly from Kentucky. They thought his choice a family embarrassment. Besides, they already had a suitable candidate picked out for him to marry. Oddly enough, out of a strong Catholic family, Mom and Daddy were the only ones to have children.

The folks had an agreement that all of the kids would be raised Catholic. As I got older, I used to think mom "sold us out," giving us no choice as to what religion each wanted to embrace. I know now that she had no choice, if she were going to be married to Daddy. I am not anti-Catholic. It took years for me to realize, that the Catholic Church did provide much needed structure for our large family. I think often of midnight mass and the large holiday gatherings. I yearn for them. The warmth, laughter of children and excitement seemed to fill the air. The death-bed vigil of loved ones when the priest was summoned to administer last rites. And how ominous he appeared, somber and dressed in black to do the duty for which he was called. How a jarring calmness would come over me, knowing it was expected of us to be unemotional little soldiers and do what we must to get through this. It was not the time for tears or emotional outbursts of anguish. Death was a time for dignity and acceptance.

The thickening odor of incense drifting in the air as we said our final good byes to our grandfather and the palm leaves that were given out on Easter Sunday. The giggles John and I shared while standing in the confessional line, often clamping our hands over our mouths to muffle the sounds.

The love and "hero worship" we had for an old priest that chose to sit with the children instead of the adults at church functions. And how intently we searched his face to make sure "he wasn't one of them," (adults) as he carefully made us name bracelets out of soft copper wire and placed them on our bony wrists, talking softly all the while. And the hurt I felt when this kind old priest was taken from us and reassigned elsewhere. John and I always swore it was because he cared more about us kids than socializing with the grown ups.

I have no animosity toward any religious affiliation. I suppose each in their own way try to bring love and understanding and families together. But I remember a lot of hurt and unanswered questions, and built up anger for treating me like a non person. And the punishment I received for daring to be so bold as to simply ask, "Why?"

Momma was a hard worker, and all of her pregnancies meant nothing when it came time for chores. I can still see her carrying a heavy pail of milk in each hand, walking carefully as to not spill any. Even in labor she worked until the last possible moment. She used to say that I was almost born in the barn. She had to finish the milking before she could lie down and barely made it to the house when I came crying into this world. Each repetition brought derision from my brothers and sisters. "Juddie was almost born in the barn!" they would tease until a fight broke out. Usually one of them won.

Momma loved babies and always seemed happiest when she had one in each arm, gently rocking them in her oversized chair, as she sang softly to them nightly. When she cooked, she always had a baby on her hip and happily hummed away. Mom was Southern Baptist and almost always wore loose fitting dresses even when milking the cows. Probably for two reasons. They were given to her, and she was almost always pregnant. She went barefoot most of the time. I doubt there was enough money to buy her a pair of shoes, but she seemed comfortable and at ease with the situation. She was the complete opposite of Dad.

The last baby was born when she was 46. I vividly remember two of my older sisters gathering up us kids and ushering us into the bedroom, putting fingers to their lips and saying, "shuuu" every time we asked what was wrong. We pressed our ears to the wall hoping to hear a sound, any sound, which would give us a clue. Finally, we heard a baby cry. It wasn't long before my sister came to the door and announced the birth of little Gracie.

John and I looked at each other with relief. Thank Goodness it was just a baby. We thought we were in trouble for dumping snow in our sister's bed and covering it up with a blanket.

John and I were inseparable as well as insufferable. He was one year younger, but we thought and acted alike. We always instigated trouble and what one didn't think of the other did, knowing full well we'd be whipped for it once Momma found out. She never really had time for us so we created our own fun and amusement. Today we would be called "problem children," but I think we just wanted a little attention. And since it wasn't given to us, we created it. Thinking back, I can only recall two times that Momma ever put her arms around me and told me she loved me.

Momma had her favorites and John and I weren't on the list. Our sister Amy topped it, probably because she closely resembled Momma. Blonde, with beautiful blue eyes and naturally curly hair, Amy always seemed to say the perfect things. I on the other hand, was shy and considered myself an ugly child. Mom used to tell me,

"It's not your fault God didn't make you pretty like Amy," or "It's not your fault God didn't give you pretty hair like Amy." John and I both felt shut out, and did a lot of things to pay Momma and Amy back: Momma for her lack of attention and favoritism, and Amy for throwing it in our faces.

Going to confessional was always a treat. We lined down the church hallway with the rest of the parishioners, whispering rapidly and comparing "sins."

"Johnnie, it's your turn to tell the priest you cussed three times."

"OK Jude, but you have to tell him you didn't mind momma seven times," John replied.

On and on we went getting our stories straight until each took a turn going behind the curtain repenting of our sins and listening to the priest's stern reprimand: "Say 10 "Our Fathers" and 10 "Hail Marys."

The next time around we just changed "sins."

Confessional is supposed to be private and secret but it wasn't. We used to giggle while waiting in line for our turn, because we could overhear the confession of Mrs. Goody Two Shoes (Momma's secret name for her.) She always whispered in such loud tones.

Once I made a reprehensible mistake. I went to a Lutheran church service with my aunt, and stood and sang with the congregation. It didn't take long to get back to Daddy. I was immediately hauled into confessional and ordered to confess a Mortal sin. The priest meted out an unusual number of prayers and I had to kneel in the pew and recite them. Finally boredom took over. I started thinking of blue skies, pretty trees and flowers, while pretending to pray. Everyone was convinced I was saying my prayers, so I guess we all won.

My folks finally decided to separate John and me. At the age of eight I was "shipped off" to spend summers with my elderly grandmother. While there, she tried to indoctrinate me into the Catholic beliefs, probably because Daddy thought he was losing ground. I became unhappy, sad and lonely. John wasn't there and I worried about him. Would he remember me when I returned? Would he change? Worse yet, would he start liking Amy?

Mom Cline (we were never allowed to call her grandmother) was a large, stern looking woman, always unsmiling, and her long hair severely pulled back into a high bun of sorts. It was easy to see where Daddy got his looks and behavior. She was cold and distant. But I wasn't there to be loved. I was there to be disciplined.

Mom Cline insisted that I say my rosary exactly at 10 PM every night. My aunt took me to counseling sessions with the priest twice a week, and 7:30 AM every Sunday my uncle took me to Mass. My reward for obedience was a treat of homemade, oversized oatmeal cookies kept in an antique cupboard with a porcelain counter top.

I wasn't allowed to have friends even though there was a home for handicapped children within view of Mom Cline's house. They shared a playground with the elementary school, however, at different times when school was in session. In the summers the handicapped children had it all to themselves. I would watch them struggle trying to ride the merry go round or swing, wishing I could go help them and meet new friends. Mom Cline watched me closely, and I was never allowed outside if the kids came out. She wouldn't hear of it! Absolutely no befriending or associating with handicapped people. That was her rule. At first I felt as though my heart would break, then I became angry. I swore that no one would ever pick my friends again, and I would never allow anyone to change what was within me. Instead of turning into a marshmallow, I became even more stubborn. It wasn't fair to be isolated from everyone except adults. I turned the situation into a game that I was determined to win.

One day I was sitting outside on the lawn and a handicapped girl walked by. She was much older than me, probably late teens or early 20's. My sad, long face must have been pretty obvious. She was the first to smile and speak. We talked and the smile never left her face. I was so happy I finally had a friend that age difference meant nothing to me. Karen left, promising to return the next day. I was so excited I felt like I was a feather floating in air!

I watched out the window for her the next day, and finally went out into the yard. I spotted her slowly walking down the sidewalk, dragging a leg, and ran to meet her. She saw me and flashed a sweet smile, waving slightly. We sat on the cool, green grass talking for what seemed like hours. All the while I would see Mom Cline's stern face appear at various windows, trying to get my attention and I chose to ignore her. This was my special day and she could just "step aside."

As we talked, Karen pointed across the street at the school. A construction crew was repairing the roof. The handsome young man with the dark hair was her boyfriend she said. He was the one that sang while he worked. I was so happy for my new friend! They seemed to me a perfect couple and surely he was responsible for her smile.

Suddenly, the shrill screams of my grandmother ordered me to the house. I went running only to be pulled inside. She was furious. The look on her face frightened me. She screamed and ordered me never to speak to a "cripple" again. I broke down and sobbed. I had finally found someone I could talk to and my friend was taken from me because she was handicapped! It was as though Mom Cline thought handicapped children posed a threat to the health of others, and that they should be isolated and banished.

Once school started and I was back home, I became much shyer and unsure of myself. It was easier to look down, when someone spoke to me.

Confessional continued along with mandatory Catechism class on Saturday's. It would take a while to get back to my usual nature. Being away from John had taken its toll. He was my strength and my pillar. Without his company and spirit I felt that part of me had been torn away and slowly the "enemy" had begun to win.

Just before Christmas, John talked me into chopping down a Christmas tree for Momma. Never mind that it was 20 below zero; we wore socks on our hands for mittens and the tree he picked out was at the very end of the far pasture. Of course, we had no snow boots so we trudged through snow banks in our lightweight shoes, sinking deep into the snow. Occasionally we would have to stop and run our finger around the inside of our shoes, pulling out chunks of frozen snow.

I believed John, trusted him, and he led me like a lamb to the slaughter. We were frozen and cold when we found the scraggy tree he had picked out as "the most beautiful one in the whole pasture." "This is it!" he declared, proudly pointing. I stood back and looked. It seemed like the most beautiful tree in the whole world to me as well.

Our hands and feet were turning numb as we began the tedious task of attempting to remove this masterpiece from its natural habitat. Several times I begged John that I was too cold to continue.

Twice I walked away getting as far as the hillside. I would hear him yell and his voice echo, "Jude, come back, I've got it chopped down." He lied, but each time I returned to him. Finally, shortly before dark, he was able to chop the thing down (a big endeavor for a little guy.) We drug it through snowdrifts until our hands and feet felt like we were walking on spikes. Our faces were frozen and numb, and the thin socks we used as mittens were matted with chunks of frozen snow. To encourage each other from giving up we sang Jingle Bells over and over during the long trek back home.

As we approached the house we began to sing even louder, hoping to cause attention to our good deed. Momma came to the door, squealed with delight, gave us both a big hug and told us how beautiful the tree was.

Sister Joanie took one look at the tree and wailed, "Mom, you're not *really* going to put that tree up, are you?"

Mom's reply was simply, "Of course, we are. It's beautiful!"

John and I beamed we were so happy. The happiness along with Momma's hug made up for the frozen hands and feet as she ordered us to take off our shoes and socks and sit with bare feet in front of the warm register. The socks we had worn on our hands had to be peeled off. The pain brought tears to our eyes, but even then it did not diminish the joy we felt in our hearts. If it weren't for John, I would have given up and enjoyed that warm register along with the hot fresh baked bread and pot of beans hours earlier.

John and I did ornery things knowing we'd be whipped for it. Still it did not stop or deter us from our sinister plans. Dad had an old pig house with a solid roof on it. We used to slip away for hours, climbing on top of the roof making mud pies to throw at Amy. Our arrangement worked quite well until one time we blasted "Amy the snitch" with too many mud pies. Her tears, fake or otherwise, put Momma on the defensive.

Since there were so many of us kids, Momma had an "enforcer" to assist her in meting out punishment: my older sister Helen, who was aptly dubbed, "Clobber." She loved to deliver punishment on mom's behalf. (Oh, the feeling of power!) Clobber's favorite form of punishment was to chase John and me down with a green willow switch that she dipped in water, generally from the horse tank and beat us unmercifully.

As usual Clobber came running when Momma saw Amy's tear streaked face and dried mud hanging on her golden curly locks. John and I had a hard time walking for a few days after that.

Momma ordered us to "Play nice with little Amy, or else." After short deliberation (about one second) John and I decided it would have to be the, "Or else." So we threw some more mud, and got tangled in the barb wire fence trying to jump over it. The beating I received that day taught me another of life's valuable lessons: Always make sure you have an avenue of escape. In later life, I would use it over and over in attempts to escape from a vicious, brutal husband.

When not causing mayhem and wreaking havoc on a quiet country farm, I would slip away to the very back pasture, sit on a grassy knoll, look at the sky and watch the clouds roll by. I don't know why, but as the sun warmed my face and the gentle summer breeze blew through my hair, I would daydream about the Southwest and yearn to live there. I had never once left Iowa. The reason I began to embrace the Southwest at such an early age is unknown to me. Perhaps it was watching an occasional western on the black and white TV we kids used to huddle around. Growing up I never felt like I belonged. There was always a void. A longing I couldn't understand. I felt peace when I was alone there in the back pasture, day dreaming about the Southwest. I began to associate blue sky and wild flowers with Arizona and New Mexico. They were "home" where I belonged. Things happen to us as individuals that we can't explain, but can accept. I choose to accept rather than question this particular period in my life, and feel peace within for doing so. It has undoubtedly affected my life.

Being raised Catholic meant that we had to eat fish every Friday. Occasionally though, Momma would slip us a hamburger if Daddy weren't around. Stubbornness has always been my curse. Given no choice on Friday fish night has caused me to dislike eating fish to this day.

My dislike of chicken probably relates to the whipping's I received every Sunday. The pact or "deal" I made with my brother was that he would help me make mud pies to throw at Amy on the condition I would practice shooting the BB gun at his favorite targets. I thought it was a fair trade off and went for the deal. On Saturday's we would slip down to the barn to stalk our prey: chickens all lined up in a row on a rail. Every time they squawked it was almost like we could hear them say, "You can't hurt us with those measly BB's, you're such lousy shot's!" Those brainless chickens were a challenge we couldn't just walk away from. Every now and then they'd squawk and fluff their feathers, acting like they didn't have a care in the world. It was a pretty disgusting sight, especially since they didn't recognize how endangered they were with two fierce hunters creeping up on them. We would take turns becoming proficient with our self-taught firearm training and nailed them repeatedly in their backsides.

Sunday morning after Mass, our job was to pull the heads off five chickens, dip them in boiling water over the open fire in the orchard, then pluck them. We hated their wet feathers sticking to our fingers and the nauseating odor as occasional feathers floated upward toward our nostrils. But that wasn't the only reason we learned to dread Sundays. Every time Momma cut the chickens up, for some reason those darn old BBs jumped out at her (must have been her keen eyesight.) The chicken's backsides were filled with small round objects and bruised severely, (sometimes we did get carried away, I'll admit.) Naturally, the green willow switch came out, but we'd slip down to the barn the next week and do it all over again. You could call it stubbornness or stupidity, but I had my reasons. One: I liked to shoot and, anyway I had to live up to my deal with John. Two: If I were going to get whipped, then it needed to be for something bad. Throwing a few mud pies didn't cut it.

There were 13 natural children in our family. Then along came number 14. We were told his mother had placed him in a basket and left him on the doorstep of a Catholic Charity Home. Never adopted, he was later sent to Boys Town. Our elderly neighbors used to "farm him out" in the summers to help with all the chores and hay bailing, until they became too old to care for things in his absence. Every spare waking moment he had he spent at our farm. At first he was just a friend, then a piece of furniture, finally a brother. His summers were going to be discontinued and all of us kids were heartbroken. I remember the day Momma told us he was leaving and wouldn't be back. All of us cried and sobbed, begging her to do something. Tears came to Momma's eyes and began rolling down her cheeks. She lifted the hem of her dress and wiped them away. It wasn't long before he came to live with us and became number 14. To this day I love and admire this man. He seldom raised his voice and never struck me, opting to stomp out the door when I had tried his patience one time too many. His kindness and patience has always remained as well as his calm, reassuring voice. He was, and is my brother.

Daddy raised his own cows and pigs and grew corn, beans and hay to feed them. It was a chilly fall evening when Momma told him she needed a cow butchered so she could fill the freezer for winter. For some reason he didn't like what she had to say, maybe it was the way she said it, or maybe he was in a bad mood. He replied that if she wanted meat, then she could get a job and pay for it herself. It was a poor choice of words. Her anger boiled. She ranted and raved, cursing Daddy and calling him unmentionable names. A few days later she announced with great fanfare and pride at a family gathering that she had found a job working as a waitress.

Momma worked hard and long hours often carrying heavy trays of food on her small shoulders. Long after the freezer was filled, she continued to work. I seriously doubt Daddy ever expected her to actually get a job. Mom's self esteem returned. She smiled and laughed easier, bought a new pair of work shoes, and almost seemed young again. Her smile, the way she patted her hair, applied makeup, always wore earrings and commented on her small ears, are some of the things about Momma I shall never forget.

It was really tough not having her at home. I guess her presence had kind of brought a peace and comforting feeling, as the smell of fresh baked bread would ooze through the air, greeting me when I got off the school bus.

As you've gathered, John and I were certainly no angels. Most of our summers were spent outdoors and our imaginations were left to run wild. We had an old tire swing, a tree house and tunnels made of hay for safety and solace. When our cousins visited we often played hide and seek in the haymow. We became quite deft as dare devils, running across the open beams holding out our arms for balance.

Daddy singled us out for most of the hostility he felt. To the community he was "Mr. Personality" and everyone thought well of him. But no one knew what he was really like behind closed doors except his family. He hated John. He mentally and physically abused him in many ways:

I would awaken to the early morning cries and pleading of my brother when he was only six years old, begging Daddy, "Please, I'll get up. I promise I'll do the chores. Just don't kick me again."

Daddy's response was to curse him even louder and call him a sissy for crying.

Momma would occasionally go downstairs and cuss Daddy, telling him to "Leave the kid alone." But her actions were never enough. My little brother was being brutalized and tormented and he had no one to turn to but me. We had no adult. We had no one to love us or protect us.

When John was seven he got a good grade at school. He was so happy, clutching the paper tightly, he couldn't wait to show it to Momma when she got off work. As usual, Daddy had slipped out that night to drink and carouse with women. Knowing Momma would be home from work at 2:30 in the morning, he always budgeted his time. He would run in, throw his clothes and shoes on the floor, and jump in bed with only minutes to spare, pretending to be sleeping soundly when she came in the door.

This night was no exception. But he had a surprise as he bounded in the door. John had fallen asleep on the couch, waiting for Momma, still clutching the paper tightly in his hands. John awoke to the noise. Thinking it was Momma, he quickly sat up full of excitement and anticipating a hug for a job well done. All he wanted was for Momma to tell him how proud she was. Instead, Daddy started kicking and cursing him loudly.

"Why aren't you in bed?" Daddy raged.

John's cries awakened me and I ran in begging Daddy to leave him alone. "Please Daddy, don't hurt Johnnie. Don't kick him again. He didn't do anything. He just got a good grade."

Just then the door opened. Momma was home from work.

"What's going on here?" she demanded. "Why are you hurting him? What did he do to you?" Her blue eyes narrowed as she placed her hands on her hips. Obvious signs of fatigue could not disguise the anger and rage boiling within her.

"Leave him alone! Johnnie, why are you up? It's 2:30 in the morning, for heaven's sake!"

I broke in half hysterical, "Momma, Johnnie just got a good grade he wanted to show you. He fell asleep on the couch waiting for you to come home." My voice was rapid. I didn't dare take a breath. "Daddy just got here. He's mad because Johnnie woke up before he got to the bedroom. Daddy sneaks in all the time, just before you get home."

Daddy wasn't sure who to hit next. Me for snitching him off or to turn back to kicking my little brother. In a flurry, he turned to John and stomped him hard, then picked him up and flung his little body across the room. John screamed in terror and pain.

Just then Momma did something I never thought she would ever do. She grabbed a shotgun and aimed it directly at Daddy's face. "Leave him alone," she snarled in a low voice, "or so help me, I'll kill you."

Shocked into sobriety, Daddy backed off. Cursing under his breath, he stumbled into the bedroom.

Momma held John and wiped his tears away. Placing a cool washcloth on swollen welts that would soon be terrible black bruises, she praised him for a job well done.

John and I knew our abuse was not ending. We'd dared to speak out against Daddy and he would unleash a torrent of pain every chance he got. We were so afraid. Who would protect us? Who would hide us? Who would care?

As I grew older Momma continued to work and was gone much of the time. The older kids were moving out to start families of their own and I had to assume more duties and responsibilities.

If Daddy had been smart he would never have challenged Momma to find a job. With Momma working nights, I had to cook for him and the others. Cooking was not then, nor has it ever been, my forte. He suffered nightly at my hands. It was a good way to pay him back for years of verbal and physical abuse.

The family complained nightly about my cooking. I tried to turn a deaf ear, for a little while at least. Their disparaging remarks and constant complaining began to get to me (it didn't take very long.) I started hatching sinister plots in my mind, over how I could pay them back.

Finally I came up with the perfect revenge, one that required very little thought. Nature's Remedies were widely used back then. Momma liked them because she always said they were much stronger than Ex-Lax (probably cheaper too.) I drilled holes in the meat of the biggest complainer, inserted a Nature's Remedy, fried the meat and served it. It worked so well in such a relatively short time that I decided to make a "hit list." I was working my butt off. If they wanted to complain, they could cook for the army themselves (and do their own dishes.) Or they could sit down, shut up and eat what was served. They did none of the above and chose to continue complaining, so in my mind, the punishment fit the crime.

I had always been fiercely protective of John. At age twelve, I began baby-sitting five kids, scrubbing floors, and doing any other odd jobs for .35 cents an hour, saving every dime. Sternly warning John if he ever needed anything; shoes, clothes, whatever, to come to me and I would help him. I instructed him to never go to the folks for anything. My, how bitter I must have been.

With all the brothers and sisters I had, there were always new people coming to the house. I don't remember which one brought Boward and Ava around, but they became leeches that I learned to fear and hate. They would come early and stay late, never leaving until they had eaten, even if that meant Momma cooking in the kitchen at midnight on her nights off just to feed and get rid of them. Momma complained plenty to us kids about Boward and Ava, but not once did she ever ask them to leave. Sometimes, she dropped hints about how tired she was but to no avail. She was ignored until she fed them, then within 20 minutes they left. Maybe her upbringing and southern hospitality was the reason she tolerated those maggots, or maybe she didn't want to incur Daddy's wrath by being as rude and blunt as they always were, even though he excused himself and went to bed.

Boward was tall and muscular, around 6'2", high cheek bones, long face and sunken eyes. He reminded me of a lumberjack with the cuffs rolled up on his jeans and brown leather high top boots. Ava was short with mousy brown hair and an over-bite that protruded beyond her punched up face. She resembled a Bull Dog, but I think the dog would have been much better looking. When she talked it sounded more like a whine through her nose.

When Boward and Ava walked in the house unannounced John and I would run different directions as fast as our legs could go. Ava would immediately run for John and try to hold him down, to plant a "wet one" on him as he struggled with all his might. Boward would run for me and do the same, while momma and daddy sat there in their ignorant bliss and thought they were "just playing" and meant no harm.

Momma's work hours changed and their visits began to increase during times when my folks weren't home. We tried to tell Momma over and over they were weird, but the reply was always the same. "They're just playing. They don't mean anything by it." Meanwhile, John and I were scheming ways to get even and get rid of them, so they'd leave us alone.

I overheard Momma one time saying how she wished they'd go home at a decent hour. She was so tired of cooking for them and having to stay up so late. The next time they came, their routine was the same. It was almost midnight and I had listened to Momma say how tired she was for the last time. Either those idiots didn't get the hint or they chose to ignore it. Finally, I spoke up and said, "Why don't you just leave. Momma's tired of cooking for you." Mom's mouth gaped open and she was at a loss for words for a second. Then she scolded me severely and told me to apologize, while she denied ever saying it.

I steadfastly refused, pleading, "I heard you say that. Can't you make them go home?"

Mom hit me with a belt repeatedly in front of them. Through it all, I adamantly refused to apologize. They sat there watching with blank looks on their faces and left as soon as she fed them.

Boward's "playfulness" and unwanted touching had become unbearable. John finally had his fill of Ava trying to hold him down and kiss him. He said he was going to strike back, and I did not doubt him. The next time they walked in unannounced and Eva grabbed John, he punched her right in the face with all his might. That night it was his turn to get whipped. Neither of us felt remorse for our actions against those creeps.

Boward was getting sneakier when he came in. He took great pains to prevent the door from squeaking and did his best to walk lightly. He was starting to leave Ava at home, as he quietly crept in during the day.

I had loosened the screen up on the bedroom window so I would have a faster escape from the pervert and often grabbed little Gracie by the hand telling her we were going to play a game. The one that could be the quietest would win. Meanwhile, I would escape out the window with her in tow, and hide her in the orchard behind tall grass for protection. She never knew it really wasn't a game and I never told her.

I can remember hiding in the bushes, fearing his hands on me, as I watched him from my vantage point, the sick grin never leaving his face. He seemed like a wild animal searching for prey.

One of his surprise visits finally took me unaware. He set upon me. I barely made it out the window, with terror racing through me. There wasn't time to run and hide in the orchard. My heart was pounding, I ran for the windmill as fast as I could go, racing up the broken steps, climbing higher and higher! Boward's long arms reached out and grabbed at my feet. I was hysterical and screaming loudly as I clung to the old steps for dear life. Oh God! Fear and helplessness gripped me. There was not a doubt in my mind he was going to harm me, as he climbed higher himself.

Just then I heard a scream. "Leave her alone!" my older sister shouted. She grabbed a 2 by 4 and whacked at his feet. It momentarily deterred him so I could reach the top of the rickety old windmill, my body swaying with the wind.

The creaking of the old steps increased terrifyingly. Suddenly, Boward turned coward. Gradually he backed down then ran like heck for the house hoping to grab my sister. Thank God she had run to safety!

I must have blocked that day out of my mind. Yet I've had a terrible fear of heights for years, never quite knowing why, until I did soul searching for this book. I visited the old farm, looked up at that still standing windmill and felt again the terror and panic of that day. I had no idea why I was so afraid until now. Now, it's over. I have faced this fear and know the reason I was so tormented all of these years. It feels good to be free.

I was in Junior High when I came home one day to find a family "council" sitting at the dining room table. A decision had been made. I was selected as the family candidate for the convent, and even my Catholic name had been chosen. As my older sister so aptly put it, "You have a chance to make Daddy proud."

I had suspected something like this for a long time. Why else would I have been sent to live with my stern grandmother? Why the mandatory counseling sessions with the priest and indoctrinations as a small child? Still I was shocked! How could they do this to me!

I screeched at my sister, Why don't YOU make Daddy proud?"

She calmly replied with a smirk on her face, "It's too late for me."

No kidding! It was obvious to me what she meant by that. The church wanted virgins!

I gave myself the choice of packing my bags and running away or staying there and fighting them. I had nowhere to go and no one to turn to, but I was determined that these people would not control my destiny. Oddly enough, if they had just left me alone I probably would have entertained the thought on my own. Even so, I felt it should be my decision for this life-long commitment; not Dad's and certainly not my sister's.

As a teen, I quietly began pursuing other religions. An older sister had left the Church many years before and was relentlessly trying to convert me to Full Gospel beliefs. She "gifted" me with an old record titled, "What a Friend We Have in Jesus." I hid in the dark closet, keeping the sound so low I would have to crunch down with my ear up against it to hear the words. If one of my sisters had heard the record or found me in my hiding place they surely would have told Dad and I would not have welcomed the outcome. Listening to that record over and over again was the first time I felt someone actually cared about me.

I was beginning to entertain thoughts of going to college and told Mom so. Mom said she and Dad would help me (none of the others had any desire to go) but laid out specific guidelines including the profession I would seek. It had to be one that would make them proud. A simple discussion turned into a big blow up. I didn't want financial assistance from them. I wanted encouragement.

I felt another option might be to join the military. My parents were furious, responding that the only girls in the military were gay. What would the neighbors think! I have often regretted not joining the military. A lot of things would have been different, including my self-esteem.

By my senior year I had a boyfriend of sorts. He was pressuring me for sex as well as marriage and I didn't want either with him. The red flags kept coming up and I tried to ignore them, convincing myself that I would never give in to pressure, that I was strong and self-assured. But that was so far from the truth. I was as weak as jelly and just needed someone to love. I wanted a child of my own to hold and love, protect and nurture. But more importantly, I needed to prove to myself that I could actually love someone.

There were nine girls in our family. We were expected to marry as soon as we turned 18. One sister waited until her mid 20's and was considered an old maid, both by the family and people in the community. With no encouragement from my family, I felt my options were diminishing quickly. My Full Gospel sister and her husband were working relentlessly on my boyfriend, trying to convert him, and me. Finally, he told them he was converted and embraced their beliefs. They were overjoyed at his decision. I felt a lump in my throat and four walls closing in. I knew I was going to be pressured more than ever to marry Bob. I was afraid, frightened and had no one to turn to except these people who so freely gave their advice.

The overwhelming need to have and hold my own child, to actually prove to myself that I was capable of love finally won out. I would never have chosen to have a child out of wedlock, so I felt my only option was to marry. I was so naïve about life. Heavens, I had never even tasted it! The "what if's" have gone through my mind and tortured my soul for years. Things could have been different, but was I meant to take the pathway that eventually led me to the Navajo people?

I told Mom of my decision to marry. Her only comment was, "Now, who's going to do the work around here?"

I married shortly after turning 18. There were no tender moments with Momma; no hugs or wishing me well. I had been in the way and a disappointment for years. It was time to leave. I don't remember being excited or even optimistic. There was never a feeling of love or really wanting to spend the rest of my life with someone. Instead, there was a tremendous amount of pressure and sense of duty.

I had been married six months when I suffered a miscarriage. I hemorrhaged badly and had to be taken to the hospital by ambulance. The horror of seeing this little blob, and knowing that someday it could have been a child still haunts me. My heart was so broken; words cannot even begin to describe the pain. I had to prove I could love, I just had to! The doctor was very kind, but I was withdrawn and hurt. He said that if the hemorrhaging didn't stop by a specific time, he would have to do a hysterectomy. The thought of possibly never having a child of my own to hold led me to some serious praying that night.

The early morning hours brought good news. There would be no surgery. That evening at visiting hours, a parishioner from my sister's Full Gospel church came with Bible in hand to visit me. I was an 18-year-old kid lying there devastated from my loss, and this jerk raised his voice and told me to confess my sins. He spoke in loud tones, almost as though he wanted to draw attention to himself, and said God took my baby because of sin in my life. I remained calm but felt hysterical inside. Then the vile hypocrite laid down a bouquet of red tulips and walked away.

My husband never wanted to work. He tried to convince me that it was not God's plan for him to have to earn a living (new convert that he was.) I had worked since I was twelve and vehemently resisted nonsense like that. I prayed it would go away. I felt trapped and alone. Bob celebrated little Johnny's birth by quitting his job the day he was born. What little savings I had, would go quickly. It was only after constant urging from his parents and brother that Bob got another job a month later.

There were so many times I wanted to leave him. Just to take my son and run away. I had nowhere I could go, no one to help me, no one to confide in. Once married always married! Those words would shoot through me like cannon! My Full Gospel sister and her husband must have suspected what I wanted to do, and began calling me often night and day telling me that God would kill my son if I ever tried to leave my husband. I was terrified! This innocent little baby had my blood in him. More importantly, I loved him and he needed me. I was capable of love; it was inside of me all along! This God that I prayed to. The record I listened to as a kid telling me I had a friend in Jesus. This Bible. His word. I read it diligently. This God wanted me to remain in a brutal, abusive relationship or He would kill my baby!

Fear, terror and finally acceptance kept me married.

Three years after my son was born I delivered a beautiful baby girl. At 5 ½ pounds, Julie was so little she could have worn doll clothes. She was absolutely perfect. To this day, she will always remain that perfect baby I held in my arms.

Juddie Cline-Lindley

Over the next year, Bob held numerous jobs, trying to convince me as well as others that God really didn't want him to work. He was supposed to preach the gospel. Supporting your family was God's business, he used to say.

When my daughter was nine months old she became seriously ill. Her blood count dropped so drastically, that she was placed in isolation. Her prognosis was dim. The poor little thing had blood drawn from almost every conceivable place on her body. When I asked why so much blood had to be drawn from my baby a nurse talked to me in a very frank manner. She said, "Let me put it this way. Your baby may not live, but what we learn from this may save another child's life someday."

I was waiting for the doctor when he came in early the next morning. I gave him an ultimatum. In 48 hours I was taking my baby home. If she was going to die, then she could die at home in my arms. He was aghast and I was adamant.

Forty eight hours later the doctor came in. I had her little snowsuit and blankets waiting. It was over. She would be leaving. I agreed to allow a parting vile of blood to be taken and waited for the results. The doctor immediately called the laboratory technician and told him to take her blood, instructing him to make the results a priority. A short time later the doctor received a phone call, and with a raised voice, said the results were incorrect and instructed the technician to return to the room immediately. The lab technician returned and I allowed one last blood sample. Once again, the technician was instructed to make the results a priority. The results came back again. The baby's blood count had more than doubled within 48 hours. The doctor merely shook his head and said, "I believe in miracles."

He signed her discharge papers and I left with my baby.

Looking back, maybe that was the turning point for me. Somehow, someday, I would leave and take my babies to safety. Even with her other medical problems, Julie suffered from a slight case of asthma, and I knew the Southwest may be better suited for her. Besides, I hadn't been able to get away from a feeling that had been tugging at my heart since childhood. I had to leave and see for myself. We had a small insurance settlement coming soon, due to damage on the house. The insurance company was going to pay us directly for the cleaning and repairs, and this would be the perfect time.

CHAPTER 3

PREFACE

When a woman runs in desperation, is she running away or towards something or someone? I was running, consumed by terror that felt like a rat gnawing a hole in my stomach with death impatiently awaiting me.

After a childhood as nothing more than a laborer within a large family, I was running. After a marriage that I was not drawn into, but rather repelled toward, I was running. After learning through my babies that I was capable of love, maybe I could have been settled in life, had it not been for a violent husband I didn't know how to cope with or leave due to fear.

I was running, but I knew I had to run. So, with my babies and my husband, who was an evil presence in my life, I ran.

I found a harsh style of life, with pitfalls and dangers that I had never imagined. By, in this strange land and among these strange people, I found why I had been compelled to run. I was privileged to find acceptance, contentment, security, a sense of worth, and most of all a feeling of being loved as a person.

What follows is the story of years that transformed my life while living on the Navajo Reservation in the barren northwest lands of New Mexico. It's a transformation that I owe to one incredible and equally inscrutable Navajo man, Kee Benally, his recognition that I belonged there on the reservation; his day by day care and concern for the welfare of myself and my children; and the power of his protection. His unwavering human devotion and friendship brought a sense of devotion to me that I had never known.

This is as much a story of Kee Benally and the other Native Americans ushered into my life as it is my own story. I came to the people as a young woman living in terror. In a sense, I never left them, because my heart is still with the Navajo. But when I finally left the reservation, I left my troubles out where there's no reason to dwell on them. The place where dust devils swirl, the sun bakes, rattlesnakes coil, and scorpions sting. It's the Rez. Home to me. A place I love like no other.

Juddie Cline-Lindley

CHAPTER 3

The Dreamers

I washed and carefully folded the kids' clothes in boxes. Knowing my trip southwest would be costly, I didn't dare spend a dime on luggage. Bob didn't want to go. Suddenly he became enthused (obviously that meant he wouldn't have to look for another job.) The day the insurance check arrived we left. I was feeling some foreboding and self doubt about the trip, yet I was so desperate to make some kind of move. My only thought was survival long enough to raise my babies and keep them from harm. The beatings Bob had been giving me were becoming more and more severe. I was getting terrible headaches from him slamming my head into the wall, and the bruises were showing now. He didn't have to worry about tearing the lining on the inside of my mouth anymore; he could bruise me on the outside. He knew no one would care and there was nowhere for me to go.

The ride was hot and tedious but the children held up well. The car had no air conditioning so I kept a cool, wet cloth to sponge across their faces. Nearing dusk we drove through Farmington, New Mexico and I spotted a canvas revival tent on the main drag, with lots of dirty trucks and a few cars filling the dusty parking lot. I stared. I couldn't understand why there were so many trucks in one place with so much dust and dirt on them.

I asked Bob to stop the car. Surprisingly he pulled in the parking lot and turned the motor off. That was too easy, I thought. Why so compliant? Perhaps it was the gospel tent and all the vehicles; new people for him to scam. Whatever his motive, I was starting to feel a sense of discovery and excitement.

As I helped the kids out of the car, I could hear voices talking a strange language and felt the goose bumps rise on my arms. Who were these people? What was going on? Instructing the kids to "stay close and hold unto my hand," we walked through the dirt into this old, patched tent.

Navajo Indians dressed in their native attire were everywhere. The tent was nearly full. I spotted a few empty chairs near the back and led the kids in that direction. Bob followed, no doubt appraising the situation for his benefit.

The women were wearing long gathered skirts with satin or velvet blouses, their long hair pulled back into an unusual looking bun. A homemade bow of yarn tied in the middle with loose strands trailed down the back of their necks. Many wore slip-on shoes or canvas tennis shoes that laced, with or without white crew socks. I gasped at all the jewelry! Stunning necklaces, pins, pendants, bracelets, rings and earrings made of silver and filled with turquoise and coral stones. These women looked like they were adorned with the wealth of the world as they sashayed down the narrow, sawdust covered aisles. Their faces were wrinkled and weather-beaten with harshness about them; plain and void of makeup, and eyes that looked like dark lumps of coal. Their hands appeared rough and many of the older ones had fingers that were noticeably twisted and gnarled. How unusual, I thought but dismissed it as arthritis and age. They walked in a way I had never seen, putting the weight on the left, then to the right; a very uneven, noticeable gait that made their skirts swoosh as they walked. Some shook my hand, with a shake so slight I wondered if they thought it offensive to find an Anglo in their midst. They didn't look me directly in the eyes. Instead, as they shook my hand, their eyes turned down or away. Low self-esteem I thought. (I could relate to that.) It never dawned on me that this was a matter of culture.

The men wore cowboy hats or baseball caps, western shirts, jeans and boots; and lots of turquoise bolo ties. Belt buckles, rings and watchbands were evident and showing. Some sported eagle or turkey feathers in their cowboy hats and wore long traditional necklaces, wound tightly with yarn around the back. They shook my hand and once again it felt so slight. Their eyes would not meet mine. I must be offensive to them as well, it seemed.

Even though the entire scene puzzled me, I felt excited and my heart began to pound. My God! I was finally in the Southwest and these were real live Indians! I was a little scared, but glad to be here. Maybe this was my adventuresome side coming out. I couldn't understand what they were saying, but what a fantastic journey already! Oh well, tomorrow would be another day and I'd be on my way. With any luck, maybe the rest of the trip would be as interesting.

The preacher entered the tent and began the sermon exuberantly. There was no shyness about him as he shouted and waived his Bible in the air. He looked around the dimly lit tent and seeing me, looked away, then glared at me almost in disbelief. I felt like sinking lower than the bug crawling on the sawdust floor. What had I done! None of the other people looked me in the eyes, so why did he?

The preacher surveyed the crowd once again, and then quite unexpectedly, told them to "turn around and welcome the bilagaana's." His voice boomed like an order a drill sergeant would yell out to his troops. The Navajo turned halfway in their old folding chairs, looked my direction and nodded, making a kind of grunting noise. There were no smiles and still their eyes did not meet mine. I had never been called a "bilagaana" before, so I quickly assessed that it must mean "white person" as we were the only Anglos there. The preacher did use the word "welcome" in English, so I figured I wouldn't have to grab the kids and run. Still, I was uneasy. I reached for the kids, clutching them tighter.

The rest of the service ended uneventfully. As I stood to leave, a Navajo man in his mid 40's approached me speaking excitedly in his native language. He was a short, healthy looking man, round full cheeks, with chubby hands and brown skin. He wore a cowboy hat, jeans, a clean long sleeved shirt and western boots. He pointed at me. As he spoke, his excitement seemed to build. Mine too. I was ready to run!

An older Navajo man stood a few feet behind the excited one. I'm sure he noted the puzzlement on my face, as I faced the two, clutching the hands of my children for dear life. In broken English he introduced himself as Kee Benally, and the excited one as Kerry Chee, his brother-in-law.

"What does this man want! What is he saying!" I demanded as I tried to move the kids behind me.

Kee sensed my fear and began reassuring me. But I was not just startled, I was scared. "What is WRONG with that man!"

Kee stepped toward me and took a moment to study my eyes before answering. There was a look of deep concern on his face. Very calmly he said, "Don't be afraid little sister."

Don't be afraid! Was he nuts! Of course I was afraid. I was terrified! I was a little white woman fresh from the farm, and suddenly this crazy Indian is pointing at me and babbling strange words that I had never heard. Where did that sorry lame Bob go? I wanted the kids taken to safety. What kind of danger had I placed them in? I had always been adventuresome but never irresponsible. How could I possibly have walked into this? Would my ignorance and innocence cost my children their lives as well as my own? Who was this stranger that called me "little sister?" I wasn't his sister! I didn't even know him!

In broken English, Kee continued speaking calmly, almost as though he were ignoring my fear. The kids were already peeking their heads out from behind me, having eyed lots of little Navajo children playing in the sawdust nearby. Once again Kee Benally tried to reassure me: "Don't be afraid little sister, Kerry Chee means you no harm. He saw you in a dream."

I thought my knees were going to buckle under me. I'm not sure if it was the words that were spoken or fright and fear of the unknown. Probably a combination of all the above. The color must have drained from my face but I quickly regained composure, telling myself over and over, "Don't show fear, stay calm."

Seeing the seriousness of the situation and the sincerity I felt coming from Kee, I cleared my throat slightly, and spoke in as distinct a voice as I could manage, "What did your brother-in-law see in his dream?"

Kee looked deep into my eyes, almost as though he was trying to "read" what was inside of me before he made a commitment of sorts. When he spoke, his sincerity rocked me to the core. Something urged me to believe and trust this stranger. Kee spoke slowly and deliberately: "He saw you coming to live on the reservation."

His words were like a thunderbolt. For once in my life I was speechless. Always my biggest fear had been that I would somehow fail God. What if God spoke directly to my heart and out of fear I would say, "I'm afraid," or "I don't want to go?" And the Lord might say, "Then I'll find someone else." Is it possible the dream of this Navajo man was somehow parallel to my own childhood dreams of living in the Southwest? Whatever the reason, I knew with such a deep conviction, right then and there, I could not just walk away.

I can't really explain what happened to me that night in that humble canvas tent with sawdust floor. I was a person that trusted no one, and suddenly in a moment's notice I was trusting Kee Benally; not only with my life, but the lives of my children as well. Kee did not know I planned to escape from a brutal husband; nor did he know my family despised me and turned their backs on me.

While Bob was hamming it up with his plastic face and phony smile, shaking hands like a white man; Kee continued reassuring me. The swelling background noise faded as he spoke. I focused on every word.

Kee offered to take us to the Navajo reservation the next day, and I agreed instantly, knowing Bob would come along. Not because he cared, or was concerned about the children's safety. He would be afraid of losing his hold and control over me. It was always about control. He went of course, if for no other reason to brag about his bravery around these fierce savages to his family.

Kee waited for us at a convenience market early the next morning. He was on foot and climbed in our car half smiling, half somber. He was a hard one to read, but looked like a man focused on a mission of some kind. The car held everyone without too much discomfort, and I had brought sandwiches and water for the kids along with wet cloths for their little faces. The reservation roads were rough and poorly maintained. It was slow going, but Kee's directions made the day memorable. "Ya ta hey to the right" or "Ya ta hey to the left," he would shout, smiling broadly and occasionally laughing, as the reservation dirt came flying through the open windows.

As we drove along, I sized up Kee Benally like daddy used to do when buying livestock. I've got a live one here, I mused. He's ornery. I was sure I had spotted a twinkle in his eyes as he occasionally glanced my way, breaking out in laughter at my dirt-covered face. Still, I felt good about the day, and more importantly, I felt good about Kee Benally. Kee looked to be in his late 40's or early 50's, of stocky build and medium height. He appeared neat and clean, wearing a long sleeved western shirt and jeans. He had a wide smile with beautiful, startlingly white teeth. This man would bring me no harm, I thought, not sure if I was trying to convince myself or really meant it.

It seemed like hours passed as we made our way on bumpy rut filled roads, reminding me of the old cow paths on the farm. Finally, we reached a little town called "Lake Valley."

Reservation life was spread sparsely. You could drive several miles before finding an isolated hogan. Lake Valley had no water supply, no electricity, no close next-door neighbors, no telephones and certainly no newspaper deliveries. Outhouses were distanced behind every hogan or rock house. This was reality such as I had never experienced!

Lake Valley

Upon our arrival at Lake Valley, Kee directed us down a small winding road and suddenly yelled, "Stop!" at a small hogan. He told us to stay in the car and wait until he returned. No problem there. I couldn't do a cut and run if I wanted to. I had no idea where I was. I watched as Kee briskly walked to the home. A small, slightly built Navajo woman with long, straight black hair, stepped outside shutting the door behind her before Kee had even reached the doorway. She was rather pretty with softer looking features than the women I saw the night before. Kee began talking, occasionally looking my way and nodding his head as he continued to speak.

Kee walked back to the car taking short, quick steps, with the lady following behind him; two small children clinging to her long skirt. I watched Kee as he walked, wearing a beat up old brown cowboy hat with silver concho hatband, worn pointy nosed black boots with silver tips on the toes. His already brown skin appeared darkened by the sun, his chubby face resembling a plump grape just before it wrinkles into a raisin by weather and age. I was in awe of this moment, this day and these strange people. Was this really happening? Why was I here? What was my purpose?

Kee reached the car with the stranger walking hesitantly behind him. "This is Suzie Juan," he said before she had even approached the car.

"Suzie Juan? Juan is a Mexican name. What's she doing with a name like that? I thought she was Navajo."

Suzie reached the car, studying me warily; her eyes darting at me but not meeting mine. Kee instructed me to get out, then the two of them continued their conversation in Navajo. Suzie continued glancing my way with a somber look on her face. I felt like I was on display. Kee read the apprehensive look on my face and took a step in my direction. In soothing tones he repeated, "Don't be afraid little sister."

I swallowed hard, and asked Kee a quick succession of questions: "What is going on?", "What is being said?", "Why must I stand outside the car?"

"Little sis, she says you're the white woman she saw in a dream twice. She saw you coming to live on the reservation," Kee replied.

Again I was shocked and speechless. I felt like shaking myself and asking where all reasoning and rationale behavior had vanished to.

When Kee told me what Suzie's excitement was all about I tried to think of it as something positive, an adventure, if you will. But it didn't work. I felt apprehensive and uncertainty. Who were these strangers? Why did they seem to welcome me with open arms? What was their reason? What little I knew about the Navajo people I had learned in less than 24 hours, but one thing I could say most assuredly, they believed in dreams.

Returning to Farmington was another long, hard drive. Kee was rather quiet, almost like he thinking real hard about something. Not once did he bring up the subject of me moving to the reservation. Every once in a while he turned and glanced back at me, his eyes meeting mine. He was different from other Navajo I had met the night before, none of whom looked me directly in the eye. Kee did. I suspected he wanted to figure me out and "read me" as quickly as possible. He had taken a chance and put his reputation on the line with the Navajo by taking us out to the reservation. What was his real purpose?

Kee pointed the way and we dropped him off at Kerry Chee's modest home before finding a cheap motel for the night. I shook some of the reservation dust from my clothes and stood in front of the mirror attempting to rub sand off my face but only leaving heavy, dark red streaks. My blue eyes stood out starkly. It would have been amusing, but I was too tired to laugh. I'll bathe later, first I had to feed and bathe the children.

Once the kids were fast asleep, I mulled over all of the events of the last 24 hours. I couldn't begin to explain the tug at my heart as I thought about these people who dressed and spoke so strangely. It was as though I was living my own dream: this reservation and its dreamers was a place for me and my children, but no place for Bob. He wouldn't last. I did a lot of soul searching that night, and as the morning rays begin to filter in, my decision had been made. I would return to the reservation and take my babies there.

I told Bob of my decision when he woke. "Maybe we can save our marriage, but don't ever hit me again," I said. He swore that there would be no more violence and I desperately wanted to believe him. Not because I loved him, but probably more out of duty and love of God. I was naïve enough to think that maybe, just maybe, he would change and I wouldn't have to go to this awful place called hell if I divorced him. My other thought remained a top priority: finding a safe place to hide with the children.

I met Kee later in the morning and told him I was ready to go. Kee didn't question me; he just appeared delighted. Kee wanted to leave immediately. I had no idea where we were going to live and there were no phones so Kee couldn't forewarn the Navajo of our pending arrival. Just like family "busting in" unannounced, I thought.

Upon our arrival back at Lake Valley, there was a home waiting, furnished with a couple of beds and even dishes in the cupboard. It was almost as though they had been waiting for me. When I walked inside my new home for the first time, a strange feeling of belonging here came to me.

"This is where you'll live, little sis," Kee said as he watched me viewing the small home with bare floor.

"This will do just fine. Thank you."

Kee looked relieved. He had been studying me closely for signs of disapproval. Finding none and hearing my reaction seemed to make him quite pleased with himself. He stood with arms folded and smiled. The sunlight from the open doorway focused on the dark freckles around his eyes. He removed his cowboy hat, lowering his head briefly, shaking the dust off and revealing thinning hair on the crown of his head.

"Mumm," I thought to myself. "OK Kee, I'll let you get by with shaking dust off *inside* my house this time. But next time you do it, we'll have a talk." I turned quickly so Kee couldn't see my smile. Only minutes into my new abode and I was already taking charge.

As the kids played and Bob paid the outside bathroom a visit, Kee took me aside and talked to me privately, assuring me not to worry about the kid's safety. "Little sister, I always carry a gun in my pocket," he said, reaching down and patting his jeans like he had a miniature security blanket tucked away. "Don't ever worry about anyone hurting your kids. I would shoot one of my own people, if they ever tried. I won't be going back to Farmington. I'll be staying close by."

I believed Kee. I trusted him. It was as though he could read my thoughts or perhaps the concern in my eyes, and was ready with an answer before I ever spoke the words.

The early days were filled in wonderment. Bob hadn't beaten me (probably out of his element,) the kids were happy, and Kee Benally filled each day with a new sight he wanted to show me. Kee would laugh freely around us and to my amusement I could occasionally see a twinkle in his eye. He wasn't shy, but then that's not something I would have allowed anyway.

Although we were a generation apart and despite our cultural differences (or maybe because of them) I was forever entertained by this usually stoic Navajo man. As time went on our greetings and conversations were spiced by the kind of lighthearted banter that I have always exchanged with people I appreciate and enjoy. Kee loved it, and came to respond in kind, but always with gentleness and affection.

The Navajo people liked it as well. At first they weren't sure how to respond to my kidding. But I never let up, never giving them a chance, and always having a ready smile.

I learned quickly to never stand "over" them. If they sat, I sat. If the elders sat, then I would sit at their feet. Even if it meant sitting in the dirt. They deserve respect and to stand and converse when they were sitting would have shown lack of it. Reverting back to my childhood and the breezy informality of an Iowa farm girl, made it easy for me.

How much of a traditional Navajo was Kee? Well, not in all ways. He was visiting one hot summer day. Julie had just disappeared out the door to play in her dirt pile with her toys, as was her daily ritual. She played alongside the house where it seemed to be a bit cooler and I never worried. After all, she was only a few feet away. But when she scampered out the door this particular day, a chill went through me. I looked over at Kee to see if he felt the same concern. He seemed undisturbed and continued teaching John about Navajo way. I heard a shrill scream and dashed for the door. My God, it's my baby! She was standing, screaming hysterically, the sandy dirt still on her little hands and clothes. I heard the ticking of the rattler even before I looked down. Next to her feet a rattlesnake lay coiled, ready to strike. The snake had probably sought relief from the heat and settled in the dirt pile, up against the cool stones of the house. Julie had unknowingly sat down beside it to play.

Kee and John were not far behind me. I grabbed Julie as she held up her arms and swung her to safety. Kee yelled at John telling him to get back. Then he mad a dash to his pickup. He grabbed an old shovel as the kids retreated to safety inside the house, shutting the door behind them.

Kee ordered me out of the way. He didn't have to worry. I wanted no part of this strange creature that appeared to jump and strike sideways in my direction.

He lifted the shovel and slammed it down hard on the snakes head. I heard an unforgettable "crunch" as the shovel hit the sand after severing the snakes head from its body.

Kee threw the shovel down and grabbed the lifeless snake by the tail. He appeared enraged as he took hard deliberate steps to throw the snake across the corral fence, leaving it to dangle.

"The smell will drive others away," Kee said in a voice choked with anger and emotion.

It was much later I learned Kee had broken traditional beliefs that day by killing the snake. Navajo believe that if you kill a rattler, some day a bigger, meaner one will come after you and find you. It will search you out, no matter how long it takes. Kee knew that, but I think he was a man who could place his own sense of duty above tradition. Later, he would without qualms, kill more snakes in our defense.

Kee spent a lot of time and patience on John. Probably because he was a male child and the older of the two; teaching him Navajo ways and beliefs, as though he were the professor and John his student. Always patient, always caring, always laughing with a gentleness and kindness about him as we stumbled over our Navajo words, and never-ending questions.

"Kee, how come you're so brown?" John asked one time.

I looked over as Kee chuckled and lowered his head shaking it gently back and forth.

"That John sure is funny," Kee said as he looked up at me with a broad smile.

"Kee's older and been out in the sun a lot more than you, John. It won't be long and you'll be looking just like a Navajo, too," I joked.

John held out his arms looking at his fair skin. "I hope it'll happen soon."

Kee broke out in laughter.

Navajo traditionally don't show emotion. Nor do they look you directly in the eyes or verbalize feelings. That's what made Kee so different. He laughed easily, disregarded our skin color and held no prejudice, joked and actually ate my cooking without complaint. Still there were never any hugs or words expressing care, other than Kee's stoic words when we first met, "Don't be afraid . . . ."

As time went on, the land and the people began to grow on me, especially after I began having visitors to my home. Traditionally, Navajo stand outside without entering, but I wouldn't hear of it. Momma *did* come from the South and was always adamant about serving someone food and drink when they came. As the Navajo came to visit I would offer them a drink of water and share food with them, and it wasn't long before I was given a name in Navajo. Translated it meant, "Water Woman."

Bob would come and go, depending on what God wanted him to do, he said. I didn't care. For the first time in my life I began to feel peace. It was such a strange word to say! With the quiet peacefulness of reservation life seeping in I had lots of time to think. A healing was taking place within me. Kee was always in the background, always showing kindness; always keeping a watchful eye on the children and never asking anything in return. He seemed happy and content like a man fulfilling his destiny.

I don't know why, and I certainly can't explain it, but the Navajo are undoubtedly the most sensory of all people. Over the years, since I lived among them, I have encountered it time and again. They absolutely have a sixth sense about others that seems to transcend time and space. Kee Benally was better at this than anybody I had ever known. Kee had his own life, of course. I never knew where, nor did I ask. But I learned that to find Kee was simply to need him. Whenever the kerosene supply began to get low, there was Kee. When the temperature got down to below zero after a winter blizzard, there was Kee. When one of the kids began to run a high temperature and I needed help, there was Kee. When the outhouse blew down in spring winds, there was Kee. When suspicious strangers began to hang out near our hogan, there was Kee. For several long years within my lifetime, whenever I needed help, there was Kee Benally.

I tried to thank him many times. "I am so grateful, Kee. How can I ever repay you?"

That always caused an uncomfortable moment. He hated me saying that because it embarrassed him. He didn't know how to answer.

Instead, I would see his face light up as he treated the kids to a piece of candy from the trading post. Seeing their smiles meant everything to him. That was the "thanks" Kee really wanted. To make others happy.

The Navajo people cared for every need. They made sure my wood was delivered and chopped. They hauled us fresh water. There was always plenty of canned goods in the cupboard. Nothing was ever said of this, nor were favors asked by any of them. John and Julie always looked forward to their visits, because as usual they brought kids with them and I provided a hasty meal with whatever was available in the cupboards. I fed the children first then sent them out to play so the adults could enjoy a meal and converse.

I always had lots of questions.

"Why do so many Navajo drive trucks?", "Don't you get *really* hot wearing those long, heavy skirts all the time?", "Are those silver earrings heavy?", "Why herd sheep? Can't they just come to your hogan when they're ready, like cattle?" Why, why why . . . it must have driven Kee and my guests crazy. Kee translated all my questions into Navajo, sometimes chuckling. The people were extremely patient while I learned. The men always gave straight forward answers without hesitation, replying in Navajo to Kee. The women would occasionally glance my way, put their heads down and every once in a while I would hear a "tee hee, tee hee" as they giggled softly, finally replying to Kee, who then translated. We all learned from one another and everyone was good natured. After all, we were two completely different cultures crossing barriers with both sides eager to learn. I often wondered why these humble people shared what little they had with me.

Late one night I began to hear eerie chants outside, recognizing in them a human voice. I couldn't see anyone out the window. Since there was no electricity, we used kerosene lanterns which really created a poor visual. I went outside to confront the intruder and found no one. I probably wouldn't have known what to do if I had found him. Fear trailed me inside the hogan. How I wished Kee lived closer! He had a gun! He'd know what to do!

My mind raced back to something Kee had told me about Navajo witchers. I believed him because I had quickly learned to have a healthy respect for the unknown, discounting nothing; just listening and learning. It was then I realized I probably had a witcher outside.

The kids had awakened and were terrified. My son cried out that he saw a hideous, wolf like creature peering in the window. The chants started again with the witcher circling the house all through the night. I did my best to keep the kids calm, while putting on a brave front. Bob was gone on another one of "God's missions," (later I found out he was spending time with an acquaintance's wife in Farmington.)

The chanting stopped before daylight and suddenly the witcher was gone. At first light I walked into the foothills, seeking a clue as to who or what this person was. All I found was a charred fire, coals still warm, and footprints everywhere. Obviously he was human, and meant us no harm or he would have done it by now. I was sure his purpose was to frighten us away; after all we were white, and living in the middle of the Navajo reservation.

That afternoon Kee stopped by and took us to Albert and Suzie's. I was still on edge, concerned and frightened; but trying to look and act brave for the children's sake. I could also feel my anger beginning to boil. An attack against me is one thing, but my kids didn't deserve this. We had nowhere to go, so the only thing to do was to take a firm stand and fight back. I wasn't sure how, but I knew it was something I must do.

We were gone a few hours and I wanted to get back well before dark. As we drove down the dusty lane, something seemed amiss, or maybe it was just a creepy feeling left over from the night before. We drove to the yard and my heart began to pound; the door was wide open!

"Nothing to worry about sis," Kee said.

Nothing to worry about, my foot, I thought! Ordering the kids to stay in the car, Kee and I searched the house. Everything seemed in order, just like I had left it with the exception of one item, my hairbrush. The last thing I did before going out the door was to grab the hairbrush and run it through my hair when I spotted any visitor driving down the lane. With the wind, dust and sand blowing continuously, I always brushed my tangled hair when I spotted company coming. A habit I have maintained my entire life, is to clean the hair out of it immediately after use. But this one day was different. I was in such a hurry I didn't clean it and left the brush laying on the bed. I had learned from early childhood to be regimental, and Momma sometimes used to make me scrub the whole wall down before I was allowed to go out and play, because she said she saw a fingerprint on it. It was almost as though I had been on a guilt trip the few hours I was at Suzie's, because I had left a chore uncompleted. I knew as soon as I walked in the door, I'd have to clean that darn hairbrush.

I stood in the middle of the room, looking around and kept asking myself, "What is wrong here?" "What is out of place besides my hairbrush?" Then it dawned on me and I began to tremble. "Kee, Kee! Come over here," I shouted!

"What's wrong, little sis?" Kee called out.

I held the brush in my hand and kept repeating, "The hair, Kee, my hair is missing from the brush!"

"Are you sure?" Kee asked, as he took the brush from my hand.

"Listen to me, Kee. I laid the brush on the bed when I left, not by the door. Kee, why would someone steal hair from my brush?"

A serious look came across Kee's face as he handed the brush back to me silently, not uttering a word. When the witcher comes after you, he has to steal something personal from his intended victim, whether it is hair, a ribbon or something else so insignificant that a person would not miss it. That's why my brush lay by the door, and the door was open. We'd surprised the witcher, nearly catching him in the act.

Kee's only reply was, "Do you want me to sleep near the hogan tonight?"

"No Kee. It's all right. He's not going to kill us, just witch us. I can't let him win. Stop by tomorrow."

The grave look on Kee's face told me that he didn't altogether agree and that if I were smart I'd be extra careful. Kee's demeanor was somber, as if a loved one had just passed away. I touched his arm and told him not to worry.

"All the witching in the world can't take me from my babies, Kee." I brought the kids in and Kee reluctantly left for the night.

Later that evening the low muffled chants began again, and I could see the eerie form of the witcher as he circled the hogan in the moonlit night. "Ya Ya Ya Ya Ya Ya Ya." The deep, throaty chants continued long into the night as he held what appeared to be a rattle of some kind in his hand, shaking it, with short quick jerks. His appearance had transformed into an animal-like creature reeking of demonic possession; the object in his hand sounded like a rattler ready to strike.

The kids were terrified, but we had to be strong. We couldn't let the witcher win. To keep calm, I kept telling myself that life is a game, and with God's help I was going to win this one! I refused to let go so fear could grip me and leave an open door for weakness. At last the chants stopped and we were able to get some sleep.

The third night it was the same scenario all over again. Finally I snapped! I was sick and tired of the chants, the fear, and above all, of wiping tears off my babies faces. How dare this evil person rob me of the first tranquility and peace I had ever known. This was war! I threw open the door and yelled like a crazy person! "If you've got a problem come into the light and talk about it, or go away!" I shouted.

Kee came the next morning, with a knowing smirk on his face; like he had a big secret and was ready to break into laughter at any moment.

"Good morning, little sis," he spoke, as he quickly put his head down trying to hide his smile.

Kee didn't say any more and didn't have to. I knew him well by this time. Somehow he was aware that I stood up to the witcher. Had he been hiding outside lying in wait for the witcher, looking to protect us? I didn't ask.

Juddie Cline-Lindley

For several days every Navajo I came into contact with seemed to be hiding their amusement from me. Kee must have told them about the witcher. He had been outside after all!

Kee thought the witcher would return and insisted I stay alert. He was right. In a two-week period, some live rattlesnakes were left on our doorstep, coiled and ready to strike. I was afraid to let the kids open the door the first thing in the morning, until after I had looked out the window. If there was a rattlesnake on the doorstep, we stayed inside until Kee got there. He'd cut off its head with an old shovel he carried in the back of his pickup and dangle the carcass across the old corral fence, saying the smell would keep the others away. At the end of those two weeks, no more rattlesnakes were left.

The Navajo began to watch me closely after that, looking into my face when I spoke as if searching for signs of sickness or imminent death. To reassure them I smiled all the more; joked and laughed openly. I had to put up a good front and let them know that they didn't have to be afraid of the witcher. After all, I wasn't. At least not on the outside. Finally, they stopped looking at me like they had just come from a funeral (probably mine.)

As time went by Kee pointed the witcher out to me from a distance, instructing me to stay away from him. The witcher had long gray hair pulled back in a traditional bun. He was thin and in his 60's, unsmiling and almost sinister looking.

"That's the guy, sis, that wanted to witch you. Don't get near him. Don't talk to him."

"No problem, Kee. I don't want anything to do with that jerk," I replied.

On one occasion the witcher came to a gathering and spoke to no one. When he walked away, the crowd parted to give him space so he wouldn't touch them. Only an evil man, brings fear to such good people, I thought.

I continued to smile and laughed openly. It wasn't a "put on" act. It was genuine. I loved these people and embraced them as my own. I was happy. I knew word had spread that I stood up to the witcher and lived to tell about it, so I was also a phenomenon.

One day the witcher passed me on the road. Suddenly he smiled and yelled, "Ya ta hey" as he extended his arm out the window. I actually think he was impressed because the little Anglo girl who stood up to him wasn't dead. Now, I might just make a formidable challenge. The witcher always waved to me after that, whenever he saw me on the road. Still I kept a healthy distance from him.

A true calmness settled over our little home after that. No more chants, no more rattlesnakes and no more Bob (at least for the time being.) Life was blissful and full of harmony. Oh, how I prayed he would never come back.

There was an old-fashioned Navajo revival meeting going on one night. When I entered (as usual the minority) with children in tow, a striking Navajo man stood behind the pulpit. He was shouting and waving his Bible high in the air with out-stretched arm. His face was somber as he shouted at the Navajo who had gathered, telling them to give their hearts to God. Kee whispered that the man's name was "Brownwater," then left me to visit with acquaintances he had nodded to at the doorway.

It was late summer. We had gathered in what appeared to be a surplus army tent that held several hundred people. The women carried their brightly colored thick wool Pendleton blankets for warmth and the majority of men wore some type of jacket or long sleeved shirt and jeans. The night was cool and a breeze chilled those walking to the gathering or riding in the back of pickup trucks. The tent had no heat and torn pieces of canvas were hanging and swaying gently from the "roof" of the patched tent.

The preacher, "Brownwater," wore a light colored long sleeved shirt that contrasted with his brown skin and bright, white teeth. He wore a turquoise and silver bolo tie (Navajo way) as opposed to a formal tie Anglo's wear, and light tan jeans fitting tight on his body. As he preached and shouted I saw a number of Navajo nod their heads in agreement or mummer softly in barely audible tones. They believed.

A large well-dressed Navajo lady sat in front. She wore a long dark store bought dress instead of the traditional attire. Her beautiful hair was worn up. She seemed to have an air of sophistication about her. She didn't really blend in. Instead she stood out. However, she did have a Pendleton blanket. That told me she may have been white educated, but had not forgotten her roots. Surely this must be Brownwater's wife.

Toward the end of the service I heard a commotion at the rear of the tent. It was two drunken women arguing. The preacher had just invited lost souls to come forward and receive prayer. He probably thought they were responding to his invitation as the two stumbled toward the makeshift pulpit staggering and bumping into people, who did their best to ignore them. Navajo way is to make unpleasant things or people "invisible" thereby avoiding conflict. Unfortunately the Navajo were accustomed to sights like this. The preacher walked around putting his hand on people's head shouting for God to deliver them in a loud, theatrical tone. I never did like to have people grab at me and frankly it wouldn't have mattered if it were the preacher or the drunks. This would be a good time for me to leave.

Being the minority in an area full of Navajo literally made me "stand out" as an easy target. I no sooner turned to leave than the drunks spotted me and immediately charged my direction. Kee hadn't come back and I would have to deal with them alone. Boy, was I uneasy! The kids didn't even have time to get up from their chairs before the drunks grabbed me. They were slobbering and grabbing at my arms and clothes. I tried to push them away but their grip became even tighter. Other Navajo did nothing to help me. After all, this unpleasantness was "invisible."

Suddenly, there was Kee! A dark look of anger contorted his face. It frightened me, yet I was relieved. Kee's eyes had narrowed with fury. He looked like a wild vicious animal ready to pounce. This was no longer the soft-spoken, easygoing Navajo I knew. At that moment he was a man capable of murder! He spoke gruffly in Navajo to another man who immediately jumped to his feet and assisted him. Each grabbed a drunk and half dragged them from the tent, while the women struggled and protested loudly. None of the other Navajo moved to help Kee, or protect the women from his wrath. That was not Navajo way. The service continued like nothing was happening.

Unknown to Kee, I trailed along behind them keeping my distance in the darkened night. I was both curious and frightened. Suddenly, I heard rapid talking in Navajo. I stopped still, hardly breathing for fear I would be detected. What were they doing to these women? I heard a sickening thud! Then another! The drunks had been thrown like dead wood into the back of the pickup. Kee started the engine. I was afraid. My mind began to race. Quickly and silently I must get back to the tent!

That night I learned a valuable lesson. I was a naïve Iowa farm girl thinking I was both "country smart" and "street smart." That sure did not mean "reservation smart." I never took anyone for granted after that. I had learned that appearances can be deceiving and even the most docile, mild mannered individual could be capable of murder if it meant protecting his family.

Kee was a war hero, a respected member of his tribe loved by many. But that night, deep in the Navajo reservation, Kee Benally became my bodyguard and as long as he had breath within him, I knew he would protect my children and me with his life. Even if it meant spilling the blood of his own people.

The next day I finally found the courage to ask Kee what had happened to the women. He chuckled, lowering his head, the brim of his dark cowboy hat covering his face in an apparent attempt to disguise what I perceived as glee. Finally, a burst of laughter!

"Little sis, them drunks sure am sore today."

"Kee, what happened? Where did you take them?"

Juddie Cline-Lindley

Kee's wide white grin spread over his face like a piece of elastic as he raised his head. There was no mistaking the diabolical twinkle in his eye.

"Sis, I drove them drunks 50 miles away and threw'em in cactus. Got lots of cactus to pick out and a long way to walk! Boy will they be sore today!"

I had become increasingly concerned over John and Julie's eating habits. They weren't eating as hearty as usual. The rule was they had to eat everything on their plates. They knew that, but lately it seemed they were picking at their food and always had leftovers. They were so good about cleaning their plates and taking the scraps out that I really didn't give it much thought.

The reservation held lots of surprises and wasn't necessarily the quiet tranquil setting it appeared to be. Everyday as the kids went into the foothills to play; I always gave them the same stern warning: "Watch out for snakes and speak to no one. If you see anyone, run like the devil's chasing you and high-tail it home." They always returned happy, dirty and tired, pockets filled with treasures (various rocks.)

One afternoon, shortly after lunch I heard the kids giggling outside. I slipped up on them, not to see what they were doing, but to listen to them laugh. I love to hear the laughter of children. If I have a choice of being in a room filled with adults or playing outside with kids, I'll do my best to be outside every time. The laughter of children warms me and makes me feel lighthearted.

As I tiptoed up to them and poked my head around the wall, I saw two mangy looking dogs eating table scraps out of their hands. Seeing me startled the kids. Their secret had been discovered! One look at those dogs caused me immediate concern. Their fur was matted down tightly into knots, and I could count their ribs, probably due to starvation and disease. The big black one looked like a large poodle with a long, skinny tail. He had a wire dug so deeply around his neck, that it had cut through the skin, and a bark so hoarse it was almost inaudible. Undoubtedly, he was trained to herd sheep, and a wire had been wrapped around his neck in place of a collar. As he grew, nobody removed the wire. Now it was too late. It would only be a matter of time. The other dog was smaller, but skinny, showing signs of starvation, as well.

"Get back away from them, before they hurt you," I said calmly.

Both kids chirped in unison, "It's ok mom, they won't hurt us. We found them in the hills and have been feeding them our table scraps."

"I don't suppose you've named them?" I asked dryly. I was beginning to feel more relaxed.

"Oh, we named them a week ago," John replied. "The big one is Rags and the other one is Muffin. Julie liked Muffin for a name."

I felt compassion and pity for these poor animals. After all, they were bringing my children joy and laughter. I could not let them be destroyed or allow Kee to run them off. The kids agreed to continue sacrificing food off their plates, so I joined in the pact.

I spent the better part of the afternoon getting acquainted with these animals feeling comfortable with them. Shortly before dark, a family drove in to visit. As they started to get out of their truck, Rags leaped toward them, showing his teeth and growling fiercely. Slobber ran out of his mouth, putting fear into me. That's when I realized that these dogs, especially Rags, were one reason for the tranquility and peace we were enjoying. These ugly, mangy looking animals had been protecting us all along.

Kee came early the next morning. The dogs were sleeping on the doorstep as he exited his truck, unaware that I was watching him. They woke up quickly. Instead of snarling and showing their teeth like they did the night before, both animals wagged their tails and ran to meet him. He patted their heads and briskly walked to the door. I was standing there with my hands on my hips.

"All right, Kee, fess up! You knew about these dogs all along didn't you? Did you put them in the hills for the kids to find?"

"No, sis. I ain't never seen these dogs before," Kee said, lowering his head and chuckling. "Must have come out of the hills to protect ya."

I was becoming more and more a part of everyday Navajo life. At ceremonies involving several hundred Navajo they made me feel like a guest of honor. They would take off their jewelry and drape it over me, or slip rings on my fingers and bracelets on my wrists. I knew I didn't deserve such respect. I was the one who felt honored and privileged to be allowed on their reservation. Why were they doing these wonderful things? Why were they setting me apart and singling me out? They had been making long traditional skirts and blouses for me, and patiently teaching me how to fix Julie's hair back in the Navajo bun, as though acceptance had set in. John was taught to herd sheep with Suzie's boys, and the kids as well as myself, were thriving in our surroundings and new culture.

One afternoon when Kee visited, I began asking questions about different tribes, the Navajo in particular.

"Kee, just how big is the Navajo reservation and why is it set apart from most of the others?"

Kee looked at me and kind of grunted.

"The Navajo rez is a big place, little sis. It goes into four states: but mostly in Arizona and New Mexico.

"Why is it so big?"

"Well, we had to make room for the Hopi people. Their rez was put right in the middle of ours so it takes space away. Course ours is bigger than others anyway, cause Navajo are special. We are chosen people, you know."

I pressed on, not giving Kee time to take a breath and feel uncomfortable. I wanted to learn all I could about my new family. Kee was patient in explaining things but didn't enjoy answering questions. It's best to learn Navajo Way by watching and listening; being patient and open-minded he told me.

"Why is Shiprock Mountain so special?"

"Well, little sis, it was one time a great snake."

"How does that make it special?"

"I told you, it was once a great snake. That's what the old ones tell us."

"Oh, I see. Well, what else do the old ones tell you?"

"They say drink Navajo tea. It calms you down."

"What else?"

"You're getting a sunburn. Rub this stuff on."

Kee talked until supper time, teaching me and the kids many wonderful things. If I didn't ask a specific question though, he didn't go out of his way to tell me. Strange though, Kee did give me a stern warning many times over, like he was trying to "drill" it into my head so I would never forget.

"Stay away from those Apaches, sis, them *mean* people."

His stern warnings worked. I wanted nothing to do with Apaches for many years, even after I found out Kee had been married to one.

CHAPTER 4

The Befrienders

Dad had passed away when my son was a year old, and I had very little contact with my family. My brother, John was never far from my thoughts or heart, and I often thought of my baby sister, Gracie. Gracie's nickname for me had always been "DeeDee." She was a beautiful child, with tight blonde ringlets that formed on her little head when the heat would cause her to perspire. She was the youngest of 14, so naturally my folks, as well as the rest of us lavished attention upon her. I'm sure Daddy's death had a profound impact on her. She's never completely healed.

Life was so different now; almost like childhood had been a blur in the wind that needed to be put aside. There was an occasional longing for Momma, but I quickly tried to suppress those thoughts; survival was more important to me. Besides, I didn't want to ever look back. I had been "trained and cultivated" to be the "Ice Queen," never showing emotion other than anger. Actually, I think my mind was deliberately making me think that way as a matter of survival. I had always been taught not to display emotions, love or affection, so now I would revert back to my childhood and all of the things that were drilled and embedded into my mind and soul would be exercised with care. My God, how Daddy would have been proud of me! I was his clone! Unemotional, unfeeling and trusting no one. I was totally isolated and that suited my family and husband just fine. There was one problem, though. I had a terrible weakness: children. I loved my children with the very essence of my soul. They were my life, and the reason I kept, "getting back up on that horse." Children are so perfect and blameless. Even bad relationships produce innocent angels that need to be loved.

I resolved that the only family I really had was my children, so I set about "adopting" Navajo as my family. Bertha Brownwater became Aunt Bertha. Kee Benally was Uncle Kee to the kids; now I had to expand my search for the perfect grandparents. It didn't take long. The first time I ever laid eyes on Grandmother and Grandfather, I knew something special and magical was happening. There was a big feast with a large number of people attending. The lean-to had been built with care, branches from trees placed across the wide spread wood on top provided shade. The fire was going and the crackling grease and the smell of fry bread flittered through the air.

This was the night I was going to learn to make fry bread, I was told, and eagerly accepted the challenge. Lesson number one was to always have the right flour and grease; which meant starting with 25 pound sacks of Blue Bird flour and big buckets of Snow Cap lard. The Blue Bird flour came in cotton sacks that had many uses after the flour was gone. One could make pillowcases, dishtowels, or articles of clothing could be made and the big blue bird on the sack just added color to our creations. The Snow Cap lard was inexpensive, plentiful, and certainly did the job.

The more the Navajo women giggled at my attempts to fashion the dough, the more determined I became. There, now I was getting the hang of it. "Teach me to fry it now," I said quite confidently, totally full of ignorance. Glances of doubt flashed my way, but I chose to ignore them. After all, if Momma could teach me to make homemade hooch over an open fire in the orchard, there was absolutely no reason I would not be able to make fry bread over the open fire on the reservation. Confidence combined with stupidity can be a dangerous thing. Lesson number 2 was to fry the dough without getting burnt. Many blisters later, after stubborn refusal to walk away and "leave it to the pro's," I finally started to get the hang of it having learned my lesson well. I didn't complain over my blistered hands and sat down to enjoy a fine meal of mutton stew and *my* fry bread. My pride must have really shown, because from that night on, I was designated to make fry bread for all the feasts, and the Navajo held me to it; delivering sacks of flour and buckets of lard to my hogan prior to every gathering.

Grandmother and Grandfather walked into the lean-to and I studied them closely, sizing them up as prospective grandparents. Grandfather had long gray hair pulled back into a Navajo bun; clean blue jeans and long sleeved western plaid shirt. He shuffled as he walked in white, high top tennis shoes, leaning forward, somehow resembling a turtle. I smiled when I looked down and saw his tennis shoes instead of the rust colored traditional moccasins. He was tall and lean with hands that looked old and wrinkled. It appeared that the veins could pop out of his skin. His hair was tied with yarn and his tennis shoes appeared new. It seemed as though he knew everyone, and virtually could walk past no one without giving a slight handshake, and greeting them by saying, "Ya tey."

Grandmother trailed along a few steps behind. She was short and chubby with a weather worn face that carried deep wrinkles and even deeper history of Navajo culture with her. She had probably herded sheep in all kinds of inclement weather since childhood, and her traditional weaver's hands and large knuckles, were somewhat gnarled from arthritis. They were rough and chapped looking, but nothing could deter the attention away from her sweet smile, and springy, almost giddy walk. She greeted friends and clan members with a, "Ya tah," and the smile never seemed to leave her face. Her long, white hair was pulled back into the traditional bun and tied with white yarn. Grandmother wore the long Navajo skirt, and white tennies with crew socks. Her velvet blouse just added to the luster of all her turquoise jewelry. On her wrists appeared old, dull looking turquoise bracelets, which contrasted with the bright turquoise and silver necklace, pin and earrings she also wore. I would never have thought that someday those priceless old bracelets would be mine.

Kee introduced me to the old couple, and even though they couldn't speak a word of English, something wonderful transpired. Their warm smiles and the twinkle in their eyes, led me to believe without a shadow of a doubt, that they were adopting me as well. Eventually we learned to communicate without having anyone around. They used their own form of sign language making it simple for me, and oddly enough, I understood. I felt so warm and almost complete inside. After all of these years, I was finally given loving grandparents that looked at my heart and soul, not my skin color.

I began to suspect something was really going on behind the scenes with the Navajo, and I couldn't quite put my finger on it, nor did Kee offer an explanation. I was having a steady stream of visitors to my humble hogan, certainly not that it mattered, but it puzzled me instead. They were kind and always brought me food, water and even made traditional clothing for little Julie and me. Of course, there was always the jewelry, too. These precious people were giving me jewelry and sash belts to wear with my attire and purses made on the rug loom. It became commonplace for me to dress in Navajo attire and the three of us were beginning to learn the language as well. I have always had a healthy respect for their beliefs, so it never became an issue, and I've never tried to impose my beliefs or way of life on them. A deep and profound respect is something I shall always have for the Native American way of life.

Grandmother began using sign language to tell me her head hurt, or where other body aches and pains were located. Then she would reach for my hand and lay it on her afflicted area. I knew she wanted me to say a prayer for her, but how could I? I felt so unworthy. I don't know why, but for some reason these people were treating me like a medicine woman. Perhaps it was the dreams of Kerry Chee and Suzie Juan, or maybe it was because I lived past the witching. I never knew the full extent of the dreams. Nobody told me and I didn't ask. Instead I accepted the love and attention that I was so grateful to receive.

When Anglo's get sick and go to a doctor they're presented a bill. When traditional Navajo get sick, they go to a medicine man or woman and pay with jewelry, blankets or money. That explained to me why, from day one, there had been such an outpouring of generosity. They thought I had been sent to them. I felt enriched and loved for the first time in my life. They taught me the simple ways and I embraced them, clinging to them tightly. Reading by kerosene lantern, using an outhouse, carefully instructing the kids: "kick the toilet first to make sure there's no rattlesnakes inside." It had all become an acceptable way of life.

Bob would come and go, spending most of the time in Farmington with his girlfriend. Generally, his infrequent and short-lived visits produced very little violence, and I was thankful for that. It wasn't for long though, and I could see the horrible evil look appearing in his eyes again, knowing it would be just a matter of time before the beatings would start again. I felt I had been given a reprieve, however short lived it may be. I was always uneasy around him, not knowing his frame of mind, and never knowing when an urge to do violence would overpower him. But for some reason, I was more nervous and became more cautious than usual. Maybe it was the look I saw in his eyes. He looked like a wild, vicious animal that had been caught in a trap. His pupils would dilate and he would smile almost like a sneer, as he would cross the room to grab me. This time though, his look was different, more intensified. I was scared, and frantically let my mind race, thinking of ways to protect the children in case he snapped. I had long worried about the "what ifs?" What if he killed me? Who would raise my kids? Who would protect them from him? If I ran away and let the earth swallow me up, would he find me? I knew my peace and happiness were about to be shattered and I was more than just afraid; I was terrified. I look back, wondering if part of my apprehension may have been fear of leaving the Navajo people.

Kee never questioned me about my real motive for wanting to move to another location. He just figured I was behaving more and more like a Navajo, and not to question was "Navajo Way." One night there was a feast with several hundred Navajo present. A very large woman who didn't look less than three hundred pounds stood up in front of the crowd and said she wanted to make an announcement. Absolutely

NO ONE would have gotten in her way. She had a commanding voice that sounded like bombs being dropped when she called me out ordering me to come to the front and stand by her. I complied like a lamb being led to the slaughter. Heck, I would have been more afraid to tell her no. This huge woman stood there dressed in traditional attire with her long skirt and velvet blouse. Her hair was dark and streaked with gray, pulled back and worn in the Navajo bun. Her face was round and broad, with huge arms and hands to match her massive frame. This woman was definitely in command and I don't think there was a man there who wanted to do anything to anger her.

I moved forward through the crowd with the kids trailing along behind, not knowing what to expect. I stood next to her and my eyes quickly scanned the crowd. Where was Kee? I couldn't find him and was beginning to get a little anxious, especially when I saw grown men lower their heads when she spoke. They didn't want any part of her either. Kee had always been my rock and my anchor. I always felt more comfortable when I had a visual on him, and he was usually close by. Was he trying to duck and hide from this woman, too?

The big woman raised her finger, pointing at the crowd, bellowing, "This woman is not white! She's Navajo! The first time I ever hear any of you call her white, you'll answer to ME!"

Sober almost somber faces came over the Navajo. I felt proud, not embarrassed. In the silence to follow my people formed a line, and one at a time, draped necklaces over me, or placed jewelry into my hands. I was overcome with emotion but this was not the time to show it. I had to be strong and receptive. I had to be Navajo.

Why had this large woman taken it upon herself to call me Navajo? In her commanding voice, why was she challenging anyone that looked upon me as Anglo? Perhaps because of the respect she had for Kee or maybe it was the dreams of the Navajo about me. All of a sudden, the door to my total acceptance swung open. Whatever the reason, I was thankful the children and I were accepted and regarded as Navajo. Our pale skin would stand out, but I was determined more than ever, to learn as quickly as possible all I could about my new culture and make these people proud that they accepted us and taught us Navajo Way.

One day Julie was bitten by a scorpion as she played under the trees. As she screamed, Kee bolted toward her nearly beating me there. Seeing the green scorpion crawling on the ground, a look of dark anger and rage crossed his normally placid face. He continued stomping on it long after it was dead, then gently bent over and holding her little hand in his, bowed his head in reverence and prayed. He asked God to "make her ok."

She tearfully cried out, "Am I going to die?"

"No little one, you'll be fine," he spoke softly and reassuringly to her. That night he slept outside, "Just in case I'm needed." he said.

Bob began coming to visit with more frequency. Upon his arrival, my son would immediately take his little sister by the hand and take her to the hills to play. I wouldn't have to say a word. They knew and they were afraid. No matter how good an act Bob put on for the kids, they knew mom was going to be hurt and they were helpless to do anything about it. John wanted to hide and protect his little sister, as well as himself. Bob's violence intensified. He didn't like the way I crossed the room, or I didn't smile when I served his food. His pupils dilated as he smashed me with his fists and drug me by the hair sexually violating me. Then he stood over my blood-spattered body grinning, and saying, "A husband can't be arrested for raping his own wife."

I'm sure Kee could see the bruises after his "visits" but would never say a word. That was not Navajo Way. But Kee didn't seem surprised when I told him I wanted to move on. Time and again he talked to family and friends, and there would always be a home waiting. Sometimes it would be a stone house called a "10-day Indian project house." The tribe hired their own people to build a small one-bedroom house with cement floor and it was generally completed within ten days, therefore the name. Electrical conduits were put into place even though there was no electricity. Perhaps in anticipation of someday having it.

When the people found out I was leaving their area, they put on a farewell feast, and once again, they draped jewelry over me. It was extremely difficult to hold back my emotions. I had to rely on my Catholic upbringing to get me through this. In the end I had to rely on my survival instincts, like I did as a child with my brother, always planning a way of escape.

If this move meant running and hiding in order to protect the children and myself then I would do it. I had no idea this would be the first of many moves Kee would help me with, and each time, there were never any questions asked, just compliance and loyalty from Kee. Slowly I had begun to know Kee; his eyes and facial expressions, his beliefs and traditions. I respected and admired this man; not because he was my self-proclaimed protector, but because of the man and person he was, both on the inside and out. At the same time Kee Benally probably knew me better than anyone, with the exception of my brother. The Navajo seemed to look up to Kee with respect and admiration, as well. He talked; they listened and complied with his wishes or instructions. It was obvious they revered this man, and it wasn't completely tribal culture or the color of his skin either. Military background perhaps? Honesty and integrity? A combination of all of the above I would say.

I never saw Kee with a woman, and he never showed interest in anyone that I'm aware of, but he probably had his private side like the rest of us. I never felt uncomfortable around Kee, nor did he ever ask anything of me. He was just there. Always close by; always checking on our welfare. I did not talk about abuse to Kee, nor would it have been an acceptable subject for either of us. What goes on in the home stays in the home. That's the way I was taught and that's the way the Navajo were raised.

The Navajo had taught my kids to make Ahjos (God's Eyes) out of yarn as a creative craft piece. Those simple Ahjos would become an important part of our lives. Every time we moved to new housing accommodations, the kids would immediately make an Ahjo and hang it on the wall, much like Anglo families hang a picture for decoration or beauty. It always made us feel warm inside and besides, Ahjos offered protection from harm. It didn't matter if we swept a bare cement floor in a ten-day Indian project house, or cleaned a dirt-floored hogan. With our Ahjos hanging, no matter where we were, our location became home.

Once again, I began to feel comfortable and somewhat secure in our new home. Kee always checked in on us, and as usual I didn't want for company. Word quickly spread and it wasn't long before Navajo were coming to my door, delivering food, water and clothing. There was always a fresh wood pile for warmth, and of course, my guests always received a glass of water and hot meal when they visited.

I hadn't seen Grandmother and Grandfather for a while and became concerned. I asked Kee to go over to their hogan and check up on them, and if they needed me, I'd be there. Kee came back the next day and said that Grandfather was sick. "No food or blankets," he said.

"Kee, what do you mean they have no food or blankets?" I asked. "I made sure they had plenty of canned goods, and I bought them blankets."

Kee's eyes cast downward as he replied, "Their nephew took them. He said they're old, and it's time for them to die."

"Kee, tomorrow morning you must take me to them."

Kee nodded in agreement. It was hard to sleep that night, worrying about the people I loved and wondering if their empty stomachs and old bodies would survive the night. I prayed, asking God not to let harm come to them.

Kee came early the next morning as promised. When I came out of the hogan wearing lots of jewelry, Kee knew what I was up too. We drove directly to Farmington. I leisurely walked around town and, as expected, Anglos stopped me to admire my jewelry and ask where they could purchase a necklace or bracelet like it. As I had done many times before, I sold it right off my body, which thrilled them as well as myself. I sold all the jewelry in a relatively short time, making enough money to buy blankets, food, and of course, Grandfather's "special treat," plain cake donuts.

We headed back to the reservation and as Kee slowly made his way down bumpy roads I wanted to yell at him, "Can't you hurry? Won't this truck go any faster? What's the matter with you? Put your foot to the floor!", but I didn't dare. I would not insult my friend, nor would I encourage him to tear up his old truck. The old truck was hot and crowded with the four of us in the cab, but Kee didn't seem to mind. I'm sure he was used to situations like this and I certainly had become accustomed to them as well. We could go slow and still have daylight.

Grandmother and Grandfather were standing at the door waiting for us when we got there. They had seen the cloud of dust as we made our way to their hogan. Oh, the smiles on their wrinkled old faces when they saw me get out of the truck. We hadn't even gotten inside their hogan with the food before Grandmother reached for my hand and placed it on her face. I knew she wanted me to say a prayer, and this time I would not tell her no.

Peering into her eyes I asked, "Grandmother, where does it hurt?"

She brushed her hand across her forehead and eyes, and looked at me, pleading without speaking a word. My heart was over-flowing with compassion and love for these beautiful human beings. I felt my eyes fill with tears as I looked to Kee for advice. Instead, he quietly and reverently bowed his head as I said a short prayer out loud for both of my loved ones, asking God to take care of them and take their pain away. I was choked with emotion and tears were falling freely down my face when I finished. Why did they trust me? Even more, why did they love me? Grandmother studied me intently and as I looked into her tear-misted eyes, she took the two old turquoise bracelets off her wrists and put them in my hand; the same old bracelets she was wearing the first time I ever saw her. Those old bracelets have become my cherished keepsakes that shall be given to my daughter when I pass.

The smile on Grandfather's face when he saw his cake donuts would have made the sun break out on a rainy day. They were both so happy to have food and blankets. Grandfather would enjoy a warm meal and Navajo tea before lying down to rest, and Grandmother would follow shortly thereafter.

I instructed Kee to report to me immediately if the nephew returned. I'm sure he had others watching as well. There would be numerous more trips to Grandmother and Grandfather's over time. Each time the nephew returned and stole their possessions, Kee and I would go to them, always receiving a warm smile blanketed with love.

Bob paid us another one of his visits. By this time, the kids and I had moved to Kerry Chee's vacant, small, crumbling adobe home but there was certainly no complaints.

The heater was situated in the middle of the room (just like the hogans) and a small kitchen had been added on. To my delight, and total surprise, there was even a large rug on the floor of the living area. It seemed so warm and cozy and made me feel good inside. Just like when I was little and my brother, John, and I would climb on top of the old shed, feeling the warmth of the sun on our faces and the summer breeze gently blowing through our hair. Our cares all seemed to vanish in that solitude and peace. That same warm feeling was what I was experiencing as I walked through the tiny home and explored the barren grounds outside.

Not far from the house was a very old hogan, dilapidated and falling apart. Humm, the original homestead, I reasoned. Quite common to find the old home and a "newer," more modern one close by. The other side of the house had long branches of firewood leaning together on end in an upright position, resembling a tee pee. Near that was the outside toilet.

I immediately cautioned the kids to kick the wood planks on the toilet before sitting down as I was wary of rattlesnakes. By this time they were used to reservation life and knew the "drill." John went exploring close by while Julie squatted and played in the sandy, red dirt. Later, they settled in to make a God's Eye to hang on the wall.

Peace and tranquility vanished and I felt a tight knot rise in my throat, the day I saw a cloud of dust coming down the lane. I knew it was Bob. He parked the car and exited with a sneer on his face as if to say, "I found you again. You can't hide." He leaned back inside the car and grabbed a rifle.

"Oh my God, he's going to use it on me," I thought, as panic gripped me and fear for my children's safety over whelmed me. "No one will ever know."

He smiled sweetly at the kids, but I could see the fear in John's eyes as he held Julie's hand tightly and half dragged her to an open field for safety.

That night he told the kids how nice it was to be a family again, as he reached across the table squeezing my arm so hard that I cried out in pain. The kids sat silent, afraid to speak.

Later, as I tucked them into bed and helped them say their prayers in Navajo, I felt a chill go down my spine. Bob was watching me closely. I said a silent prayer to God, asking him to let the children sleep soundly so they would not witness the brutal attack I knew was coming. God heard my prayer.

Bob beat and violated me. Then with blood running out of my mouth, he grabbed the rifle and shoved it hard into my stomach, his finger on the trigger.

"I could kill you right now, and no one would ever find you," he said. "I haven't made up my mind yet. But think about what I'll do to the kids, with you out of the way. The guns loaded and I'm going to lean it up against the wall," he sneered. "Let's see if you've got the guts to try and shoot me. I'm going to sleep next to John tonight. Just remember, if you shoot me, you might hit him, too."

I crouched in the dark corner on the floor, doubled over in pain all night. Many times throughout the night, I stared at the rifle as the moon filtered light on it through the small window. Oh, how I wanted to destroy him and remove this horrible pain and threat from our lives. Then reality hit me. What if I accidentally hurt my son?

Kee came the next morning. John saw the dust flying and yelled, "Kee's coming. I see the dust ball!"

I limped into the main part of the house and put on a long sleeved shirt to hide my marks. My head was so sore I couldn't comb my hair or hide the marks on my face. I kept my head down with no eye contact and minimal interaction, avoiding him as much as possible.

Kee stayed a short time before calling out, "I'll be here early tomorrow morning, sis."

I stood to one side of the window watching as my friend tousled John's hair on the way to his truck. Kee knew. That's why he deliberately said he would come tomorrow. Kee came every day. He just wanted to remind Bob.

The kids played hard and went to bed early. It was hot with no breeze blowing, so Bob opened the door. I just finished doing dishes by kerosene lantern when Bob whispered, "Did you see that? There's someone out there."

I looked up to see two silhouette shadows jump behind the old hogan.

"Where's my gun? I'm going to shoot them," Bob shouted.

The silhouettes were clearer now, and appeared to be small, slightly built young men wearing cowboy hats. They bobbed their heads out from behind the hogan and jumped back for cover. They had been discovered!

Suddenly they sprang for their horses. I heard the sound of a metal can clanking as one kicked it in haste. They mounted their horses and tore across the barren land at full gallop.

Bob stepped out the door and aimed the rifle squarely at the back of one of them. "I'm gonna kill him, and teach them both a lesson," he growled.

I grabbed the gun and with all of my might and pushed it off to the side just as he squeezed the trigger.

"Look what you've done, you stupid woman. I coulda had him!"

"My God, Bob! It was probably a couple of teenagers trying to siphon gasoline. Didn't you hear the sound of the metal can?"

He smacked me across the face knocking me down into a tumbleweed.

"You ruined my fun," he spat out as he walked back into the house.

The next morning Kee returned. When told about the two young men, he looked alarmed and walked outside checking for tracks. He found an old gas can near the hogan, shook it, and took the lid off to smell. Then he checked Bob's car. Gas had been siphoned, probably from the two teenagers, Kee reckoned.

"Sis, are you and the kids all right?" Kee asked.

"Yes, Kee," I replied. "I thought it was kids."

"I'll look into it. Don't worry. I'll sleep outside tonight. Tomorrow I'll get to the bottom of this."

I felt relief. Bob wouldn't hit me tonight.

Kee disappeared early the next morning, returning before noon.

"I found the thieves," he said triumphantly. Still a look of agitation and embarrassment shown on his face. "Two brothers, over the hill," he said, nodding toward the east. "Twelve and thirteen. Needed gas to sneak off to a Navajo dance. Thought they'd take their dad's truck, too, 'cause he wasn't using it at the time." He glanced at Bob and said "Good thing you used your head and didn't shoot them kids."

I walked Kee to his truck a short time later. Quietly he said, "Don't worry about them boys trying to bother you, sis. Their dad's taking care of them," he chuckled.

The kids had friends and easily made others wherever we lived. My son was close to three brothers and visited them often. When he wasn't with them, much of the time their folks were visiting us. Instead of trying to remember all of their names he simply referred to them as, "The Bisti Boys."

One day John had spent the better part of the day over there and I went to pick him up. They lived in a hogan with a window near the door. As I approached, I could see John sitting in the open window, with the Bisti boys peeking and ducking their heads in laughter every time he called out to me. "Hey mom," he shouted, "Doya shona bilagaana." Oh this was wonderful, I thought. These boys are helping John learn his Navajo. But why was I so suspicious? Maybe it was the laughter and the ducking of heads. Or maybe, it was the obvious blush on their parents faces as they stood at the doorway.

"Ok, guys. What's the joke? What does it mean?" I half laughed as I waited for a reply, and my eyes turned to their folks. The parents were both large, having been well fed on mutton stew and fry bread. At first glance, if you didn't know Navajo culture, you'd think they'd both be assertive, because of their size if for no other reason. Finally, amid the laughter, the boys "fessed up." Translated, doya shona bilagaana means, "no good white man." Of course they wanted John to say it. Courage and culture would have prohibited them from saying such things at their young age. We all had a good laugh, and as we were leaving, John crawled over me to hold his head out the window, waving and shouting, "doya shona bilagaana," over and over again.

Another day the Bisti boy's parents came to visit and of course, I gave them a drink of water. But today was going to be different. I wanted to cook them something special. They sat and patiently waited while I cooked one of my favorite dishes; spaghetti. When the meal was ready, I asked them to come to the table and piled their plates high. They looked at each other, then looked back down at the heap of spaghetti on their plates and dug in. They ate every last bite; kind of grunted, pushed themselves back somewhat from the table, and belched loudly in appreciation. I was highly amused and wanted to laugh, but knew now was not the time.

Bob was relentless in following us. Having little knowledge of the reservation was not a deterrent. He would simply ask around for a white woman and kids. Since we were probably the only ones around, other than the occasional trading post owner, he managed to find us even in the remote areas. It was the same everywhere we went. He would show up with no warning, striking fear into us. John would grab his sister's hand and run and Bob would severely beat and violate me before leaving. As he half sneered, half laughed, his parting words to me were always that he'd kill me if I ever tried to leave him again. After he was gone, I always prayed it would be an eternity before he returned.

There were times when I must have really wanted to confide in Kee, but couldn't. "What goes on in the home, stays in the home." Those words echoed in my ears, and were embedded in me since childhood. I could not speak of the pain and suffering at Bob's hands, and even though it may sound strange, all I ever wanted was a family, and if God could just "straighten" him out, maybe there was a chance. A chance to have that "fairy tale" family where people are treated with love and kindness.

I would never have disrespected Kee by asking him to become involved, nor embarrassed myself. I knew Navajo way was not to get involved in domestic problems. Anyway, maybe they thought this was acceptable behavior for Anglos.

I continued to stay on the move and run and hide, always hoping and praying that someday I would be set free.

One day Kee visited, and said he had a surprise for John and wanted us to go with him. He took us to a hogan I had never seen, instructing us to remain in the vehicle while he went inside. He was in there for only a short time before he came out and disappeared behind the hogan out of sight. He emerged carrying the ugliest creature I believe I have ever seen, but judging from the broad smile on Kee's face, I knew I better keep my mouth shut.

"Here John, this is for you," as he proudly held "this thing" out to my son. I could scarcely hide my disgust and puzzlement. Kee said, "It's all right, little sis. It's a coyote pup for John. He needs a dog."

Kee was not one to argue with, nor would I have said a word. The look of excitement that crossed that little boy's face when he held that coyote puppy was sheer happiness and joy. I would never wish to take that from him. John chose to name him "Mahe" which translates to "coyote."

The puppy took to John in short order, and it was no wonder. John fed it scraps from his plate and slept with the pup in his arms as he lay in his sleeping bag at night. As the coyote began to grow and claim more of his surroundings, he became a thief of sorts. When John slept, the animal would steal everything within reach, which once included a five-pound sack of potatoes, and drag or carry those objects in his mouth. It literally surrounded John's body with them while he slept. Then the darn thing would form a ring of pee all over it. When I got up I would find John sound asleep with this bigheaded creature in his arms, and his little body outlined with all the pee soaked objects stolen the night before.

Kee had cautioned us that coyotes have a "blood sickness" and don't live much longer than a year. He said they would start bleeding from the nose and then die. He figured the pup might live a year or even a year and a half. We knew this and accepted it as part of reservation life long before John was ever presented with this gift. John liked to carry the puppy in his young arms everywhere he was allowed, and easily took offense whenever someone made a comment about the size of the dog's head, which seemed unusually large. Kee always said the dog's body would catch up with his head and eventually it did. As the coyote grew he would sit in the middle of the floor with head tilted up and howl a blood curdling sound. It used to make my hair stand on end and I could never get used to it.

No running water meant baths were given in a basin. We also had a communal bathhouse with a brick wall between the men and women, but I felt unsafe there. When I washed my hair in the communal bathhouse, it always came out smelling and feeling dirtier than when I went in; almost like the smell of oil. I asked around about the water supply and learned that a company was digging for oil but struck water first, and was not allowed to continue digging, so a bathhouse was built. Though this was never verified, I think the story was true. It sure smelled like oil.

There was a hot springs of sorts in Bisti. Warm, clean water flowed year round. It was wonderful. The big drawback I was told, by the Indians, was that you couldn't drink it. If you did, more than one warned, you would get a bad case of stomach problems. It smelled so good, fresh and clear looking, that I got tempted and filled some jugs, taking it home with me. We drank it and I cooked with it, all the while telling myself that something that tasted that good couldn't possibly be bad. Boy, was I stupid! We got stomach problems, all right! A better term was diarrhea! Making a dozen trips to the outside bathroom in the middle of the night, we each took our turns waiting, and yelling at the lucky one inside, "Hurry! Can't you go any faster!" I've gotta go!"

I learned a good lesson, and NEVER brought that good smelling, clear water home again.

Kee was very proud of his military background, as are most Navajo. Their exemplary behavior under fire is unquestionable. He often talked about the Navajo Code Talkers and would laugh heartily showing a wide smile with beautiful white teeth as he declared, "The Navajo Code Talkers won the war. Those other guys didn't know what we were saying; they didn't know Navajo."

I have not proof or verification that Kee Benally had been a Code Talker. Perhaps he was just proud of his people and proud of being a Navajo. Most definitely he felt honored to have served his country.

CHAPTER 5

Beads of Cedar

On the move again! This time Kee borrowed a tiny trailer from someone and moved us to Pinon, parking the trailer on the Yazzie's homestead with their permission. The Yazzie's were warm, hospitable people who treated us kindly. We were near the so-called disputed-land boundary line, and often the Yazzie's and Kee would sneak us over the fence line to show us "Navajo secrets" and treasures.

Undiscovered ruins, pottery shards, arrowheads and grinding stones seemed to be just about everywhere. This is Navajo land, I was told. The old ones were born and raised here, and now the government had put a fence across it, dividing the land up so a portion could be given to the Hopi. The Navajo were told that many of them would have to move. This included elders who had lived on and toiled the land for a lifetime. Some would have to leave their deceased loved ones behind and, just as importantly, vacate sacred ground which was protected by Navajo spirits.

Kee had warned me that it was a bad area for witchers, or "skinwalkers" as they were called by local Navajo. Others confirmed it as well, but by this time I felt seasoned and ready for battle. I didn't try to tell myself that I was invincible; I had learned that only a very foolish person would do that.

This was rugged, untamed land that had changed very little over the centuries. Indians dipped drinking water from the running streams, used natural herbs as medicines, and traditional sweathouses for cleansing. Homemade rug looms could be seen in almost every hogan. Oh, how I remember the smell of the fresh crisp, mountain air early in the morning, and the aroma of sizzling steak frying in the cast iron skillet and fresh coffee brewed over the open fire, rising in the air and beckoning me.

By all appearances it was a beautiful dream world, unspoiled and untouched for centuries. But inwardly, mysticism, spirits, and evil lurked. It was thrilling and exciting to be there, at the same time a little frightening. There was a sense of adventure tempered with caution. The beautiful mountains and hills called to me. The cedar trees would sway to the breeze, as the "secrets" of the land remained intact. Gradually, as trust began to build (with Kee's assistance, I'm sure) the Navajo showed me some secrets the land had hidden.

"Come here, sis," Kee called to me one day. "I want to show you something." I followed after him as he clambered on top the mound. "Look around, what do you see?"

"Well, the sky is pretty from here," I said ignorantly. "Is that what you mean?" The scowl on his face let me know immediately that the pretty sky was not what he had in mind.

"Look down by your feet," he instructed impatiently. "Now, what do you see?" The toe of his boot moved the dirt around.

There were pottery shards everywhere blended in with the dirt. I had been walking over these ancient relics without even knowing it. Some were large pieces of broken vessels that could easily have been pieced together. History was here and I was privileged to witness it. I carefully picked up some large pieces and after studying them intently, gingerly lay them back on the ground, so as not to disturb Mother Earth. Kee watched my actions carefully and as usual, never said a word. That meant he was pleased. I had done the right thing by giving the pottery back to Mother Earth.

"There's another old place under this one," Kee said.

"Another what? Another village?" I asked, searching Kee's face for the answer.

Kee nodded his head and said yes, in Navajo, which was the only response I received as he drew his lips into a pouting position and used them to motion with, much like Anglos use their fingers to point.

The day was full of total amazement. Yet other Navajo promised to take me to even more secret locations the next day.

Next morning the kids and I were up early and ready to go exploring. There's no way I could have slept in anyway, with the aroma of steak and eggs filling the air. Since there were no cattle around, I wondered where the beef came from, but figured it was none of my business and kept my mouth shut. The Yazzie's had a large extended family living on the property in various hogan's, so there was always lots of company and plenty of kids for John and Julie to play with. Still, in the back of my mind, I remembered Kee's warning about the skinwalkers. I wasn't about to let my guard down. Today would be another memorable day, I was sure of it.

Edison was our self appointed guide and eager to show us sights very few, if any, whites had been allowed to see. He was tall and muscular, with dark hair and complexion, probably in his middle 20's. How striking, I thought, until he smiled and showed the gap where his front tooth had once been. A little dental work and his wife would have a hard time keeping the girls away from him. He was friendly and outgoing. He and Kee seemed to hit it off pretty well, conversing in Navajo and laughing and talking amicably.

We followed Edison as he led us up the mountain until we came to a barb wire fence. There were "No Trespassing" signs posted up and down the fence line, as Edison explained the government put them there to keep Navajo away. So this was the infamous disputed fence line!

Edison glanced over his shoulder at us and laughed as he crawled on his belly and went underneath the barb wire to the disputed side.

He held up the razor sharp wire until each one of us had crawled under, making it very plain to me that this was still Navajo land and no one was going to keep him out. He climbed over rocks with ease as the kids and I slowly made our way in his direction with Kee occasionally glancing over his shoulder checking on our welfare. Edison finally stopped at what appeared to be a cave entrance. Grinning broadly he instructed me to crawl in on my stomach.

"No way, I'm chicken! I'm afraid there might be a snake in there. Kee, you go first."

I didn't have to say it twice. Kee was on his belly and crawling in. He came out a little while later, and the look of tranquility and amazement on his face is hard to describe. It was almost like he had seen a vision or spoke with a heavenly being.

Softly he said, "I've heard about this place and I've waited 20 years to see it."

That's all I needed to hear. I was down on my stomach and away I went. It was spectacular! Not beautiful, but awesome. Inside the cave was the huge head of what appeared to be a petrified dinosaur. Its features were very distinct. At its mouth lay a bowl of hard corn kernels. I exited, shaking. I listened to Edison explain how the Hopi medicine men were bringing the creature corn for food and praying over it, feeling that it was sacred. The scratches on the nose area were from medicine men scraping on it to mix with their prayer medicines.

We left the cave and I knew with a certainty I would never be able to find my way back there, nor would I care to. I've seldom talked about it in 30 years.

We began to see headlights late at night high up on the hill. The coyote's incessant howling woke us all and we found ourselves gathering outside, wondering who would be driving up there so late at night, and why? I could sense something was wrong before any words were ever spoken. Edison's younger brother had been sleeping outside on a cot, due to the heat and cramped living quarters in the hogan. By morning he would roll up in blankets as the cool mountain air set in. We discussed the headlights and the howling. I noticed the young man had a look of fear on his face. In fact, worry and concern shown on every face. Then it was decided: A skinwalker was sneaking around. That explained the headlights where normally vehicles could not go, and the wailing of the coyote. The skinwalker was transforming himself into the coyote to witch us. No one was sure who his intended victim might be, so the elders put everyone on alert to protect each other.

The men got their rifles and shotguns ready. As nights passed, Edison's younger brother continued sleeping outside on the cot with the shotgun resting on his arm. How brave for a 14 year old, I thought, especially when the fear was so evident. He woke late one night to a wolf-like creature peering down at him. Screaming loudly he grabbed for his gun. Then the creature disappeared into the night. Everyone woke to the screams, and with whoops and hollers, came running, rifles in hand. Excitement and anger filled the air! How dare this evil one violate their home and tranquility! Quickly they formed into small groups and spread out searching for the witcher, each one checking that his back-up was close by to ensure they would not fall prey to the evil one. Even though we spent hours trying to track him, the prints disappeared on the hillside.

Was this a figment of the imagination, or was it real? The Navajo believed it to be real or they would never have put themselves on alert and slept with their rifles. The footprints were real. So were the car tracks where no vehicle should have been, or normally could have driven. The coyote's howl was real. How was this to be explained? The Navajo believe in keeping things simple. They told me it was a skinwalker, or witcher if you will, and I would never have disputed it then, or now. Whomever or whatever this "thing" was that appeared, struck fear into the people, but created no panic. The creature was not ready for the outcome. Instead of mass confusion, the men complacently loaded their rifles and waited for his return.

A few nights later, at a gathering, the Navajo women lined up and put so many necklaces strung from cedar beads over my head, that

I quit counting. Strange, I thought, necklaces made of cedar beads instead of silver. Must be the area. It didn't matter to me anyway; I was thrilled to be given gifts. They came from the heart, they were handmade and they were beautiful. What more could a person wish for? Some were elaborately strung designs woven with intricate detail, and others were long and plain with minimal numbers of glass beads added for color. How creative to use things made from nature itself. I would never have guessed cedar beads could have been used for jewelry. Nor would I have guessed the symbolic meaning of wearing something made from cedar seeds.

Years later, I found out I had been witched and the people were putting cedar beads or "ghost beads" as the Navajo call them, around my neck to protect me. Kee and the others didn't want me to worry unnecessarily, so I was never told.

I did know at the time that they were all bearing arms and it would have been a great honor for one of them to shoot a skinwalker. That would have been talked about around the open fire and the person that destroyed the evil one would have been revered.

I had met such a hero, a kind of legend in his own time: Hoskie was a large Navajo in his 20's. Over-weight from all the fry bread, his chubby fat jiggled when he walked. His bright smile with shiny white teeth flashed indiscriminately at anyone willing to sit and listen to one of his jokes. How unlike the more traditional Navajo whose world was a stark reality of hardship, without a lot of humor.

Hoskie lived in a hogan with his wife and two young children. He didn't work and preferred to lie in bed much of the time in the open hogan area. The door remained ajar so he could catch the soft, cool mountain breeze, making things more comfortable for him. His wife didn't seem to mind. She stayed busy with her rug weaving as the children played nearby.

Because of his size I never called him Hoskie. I felt the more appropriate name for this jokester was "Husky." Nodding her head in approval among giggles of laughter, his wife gave me the "go ahead," as I renamed him at the campfire one evening.

Husky enjoyed his new name and the attention he received. One day as Kee and I approached his open door hogan, I saw a thick leg swing off the side of the bed followed slowly by another. I stood outside and yelled, "Get your lazy self up, Husky. I'm here to visit." Pretty soon he came bounding out filling the frame of the doorway with his large body. A wide smile covering his face.

I heard Kee laugh and looked up to see the delight on his face as Husky's wife and I kidded him unmercifully. Husky had teased everyone for so long, and now a strange white woman was helping to put him in his place.

My fondness for Husky and his wife was obvious, especially to Kee. Nothing got past him. He always stayed in the background carefully watching the three of us as though he was our self appointed protector. Kee felt he could completely trust me or he would never have taken me aside and told me the truth about my friend, Husky. That was long ago, so I feel now the story can be told.

"He was 14 when he killed a skinwalker," Kee said. "Hoskie was living with his folks in a hogan not far from here. One night a skinwalker came bent over and walking on all fours. He was wearing a coyote skin and entered their hogan to steal. Hoskie's folks sat still, afraid to move or look in his direction. The skinwalker stole things from them and left. Hoskie was young. And mad. He grabbed the rifle and shot at the skinwalker, wounding him. The skinwalker ran fast, throwing the coyote skin down. But Hoskie followed the trail of blood. He's a good tracker, Sis." Kee lowered his head shaking it as he laughed heartily.

He continued with his story. "Hoskie tracked that crazy man to his Hogan door. The skinwalker's wife came to the door and told Hoskie to "go away," her husband was sick. But Hoskie wouldn't leave. He walked right in that door and went over to the bed. The skinwalker was sick all right. He was dead!"

It was obvious there was more to my friend, Husky, than I would have imagined. This friend and jokester thought nothing of shooting "the evil one" down without fanfare when his family was threatened.

Kee finished his story by telling me the skinwalker's wife buried him quietly on the reservation. She told people he had died of a heart attack. That was *her* story and she wasn't going to change it. She made no attempt to explain the trail of blood and lived in seclusion the rest of her days.

Hoskie on the other hand, became revered by tribal members for his bravery. He had saved his family from the evil skinwalker, thereby protecting others as well. No wonder the Navajo laughed at his corny jokes. This man could do no wrong.

A reader may think this skinwalker episode is much ado about nothing. But the legend of skinwalkers lies deep in the psyche of the Navajo people. Much of it has never been and hopefully never will be written down. To them, a skinwalker is the embodiment of evil, starting with the ritual of cloaking themselves with the coyote skin. Any telling of the entire story would deeply offend the Navajo people, and bring dishonor to me.

Even after leaving the reservation I carried a small string of cedar beads in my medicine bag, or occasionally wore a necklace strung from the seeds that had been given to me so long ago. When I went into law enforcement, I put some in my pocket while on patrol duty or placed some in the glove compartment of my vehicle. The other officers didn't find this unusual behavior at all. Several were doing the same. You see, when you live among the Navajo you quickly learn to have a healthy respect for their beliefs and the unknown. Call it superstition if you like. I call it Navajo.

CHAPTER 6

Leaving the Reservation

Time was fast approaching for me to leave my beloved people. I had such fear of Bob, of being stalked and beaten. My safe haven was dissipating like vapor in the wind. It would soon be time for my son to attend school and maybe, just maybe, it was time to take the things I had learned and move on. Peace, harmony, tranquility; being as one with nature, Father Sky and Mother Earth, all this and more could never be taken away. My people had taught me well, and over the years when things have gotten troublesome and I need to sort things out; I always retreat to the reservation. There I find peace and the answer I seek.

Kee never openly said he knew why I wanted to keep moving from one area of the reservation to another. He never questioned me. Instead he looked at me with a somber face every time I told him I wanted to leave an area; as though he were studying me, but yet there was no inquisitive look. I told Kee it was time to leave Pinon and he didn't seem surprised. He left for a few days and came back to let me know he had found a family that would let the kids and me live in a spare hogan. The small trailer was returned to its owner and we left for the Lake Valley area, where I set up housekeeping once again.

One day Bob showed up at our hogan. He began crying in front of the children; about how much he loved me and how we had to be a family. He was sober, his eyes weren't dilated and he appeared so sincere and remorseful. The kids were upset, probably with fear that he would come back again, and I was upset, with my Catholic background reminding me what a failure I would be if I didn't give him another chance. Against my better judgment and uneasy feelings, I told myself I just had to try one more time. Bob wanted us to go into Farmington and spend the night to plead his cause. Like a naïve fool I packed the kids up and went.

Shortly after arriving in Farmington and unpacking at a newly built motel, (I shudder to think where he got the money to pay for it) he told the kids to go for a walk. I felt a lump rise in my throat but calmly put on a brave smile for the kids, encouraging them to explore the motel. I knew what was about to happen and I didn't want my babies to witness it.

Bob's pupils were dilating, (he used to say the reason his pupil's dilated was because he was coming down off the anointing) and I knew he was going to beat me. He tricked me with his more sincere approach, and by using the kids and church. He was going to make me pay a big price for hiding and staying on the move, making it more difficult to find me. I had no idea just how great that price was going to be.

The kids had no sooner shut the door than he grabbed me by the throat with his massive hands. He literally picked me up and slammed the back of my head repeatedly into the cement wall. He would stop only long enough to hit me in the face, and the whole time he had a sinister smile on his face. Blood was running everywhere and I remember sinking into a heap on the floor. As I started to lose consciousness he grabbed me by the hair and drug me into the bathroom, throwing me clothes and all into the shower. His only comment was, "We can't let the kids see you like this, now can we?" The sneer that never left his face haunted me until I wrote this confessional.

When the kids got back, blood was explained as spilled ketchup. He told them, mom had a bad headache after slipping and falling on the wet bathroom floor, and was lying in bed because the darkened room felt better on her eyes. My poor babies! I could only groan, but

Juddie Cline-Lindley

out of fear for their safety I would have kept my mouth shut anyway. I was badly bruised and could hardly walk as we left the motel room the next day. He took us back to the reservation and moved back in so we could be a "family" once again. Physically I was helpless, mentally and emotionally I was drained. The only thing(s) that kept me from praying for death was my babies, and fear of what he might do to them.

He left for a short time after that, coming back a few days later announcing he had rented us a trailer in the Arizona desert. Kee knew what was going on (I steadfastly had never said a word,) but was bound by tradition and did not intervene, nor did I ask him to. Besides, he knew I was not going to allow my son to be shipped off to a boarding school, as we had discussed it many times before.

With much sorrow I told my family goodbye. Until then I did not realize the pain and anguish that cut deep into my soul over the "loss" of telling loved ones goodbye. In my heart I felt it was a final farewell, and I knew I could never look back. I could never return to my beloved reservation or to my family and friends again. I could never see Grandmother and Grandfather again. Oh God, how I would miss their smiles, and worry about their pain. I would never see Albert and Suzie again; fuss over my Navajo guests as they would come to my hogan for a spaghetti meal, never see Kerry Chee's shy smile again, and more importantly never see my friend and rescuer, Kee Benally, ever again.

The mixed emotions, heartache and pain over leaving is something I swore to myself I would never experience again. To this day, I don't like getting close to someone; I can be very reclusive to self, always want a "safe place" and absolutely hate to say, "goodbye."

I knew I was leaving the reservation, but the reservation would never leave me. That was the one solace that gave me peace. No one could take it from me; not then, not ever.

Our new desert home was a beat up old trailer with a broken swamp cooler. The temperature would easily reach 115 degrees and above with no hint of a breeze. I would give the kids showers three and four times a day trying to cool them down. Little Julie would sometimes cry because the water coming out of the cold facet was so hot it would burn her delicate skin. Sleeping at night was fitful at best. The desert was a miserable place to be in the summer. Anyhow, I knew my heart would always belong on the reservation.

Bob quickly moved us to a succession of homes, each just as bad as the first. He seldom worked, citing God as the reason once again. I was allowed to eat one meal per day unless he decided he wanted that, too. I was never reluctant to give him my food; only feel fear if I didn't. Besides, if my kids were being fed, somehow, someway, God would keep me alive.

Christmas had always been a real hard time for me. My mind would reflect back to when my son was a baby. There was no money for presents let alone a Christmas tree or lights. One night in response to my begging and urging, Bob drove around the streets in Des Moines, Iowa. I wanted to show my son the twinkling lights and teach him the magical feeling of Christmas. I was so sure I could make him understand, even if he were a baby. Part of the reason I begged to go, was probably for myself as well. Growing up in a large Catholic family, Christmas brought excitement and even loss of sleep, worrying whether Santa would forget me. I remember my folks had friends who always gave them a huge tin filled with cookies and candies at Christmas. Oh, it was wrapped so pretty! My brother and I figured that when a large package arrived from their friends, it was the tin of candy. After all, it had been so for three straight years. We plotted how to sneak into it and wrap it back up so Momma would be none the wiser. When Momma went shopping leaving John and me alone we seized the opportunity. We got a "little" carried away as we tore at that lovely Christmas wrapping, still convincing ourselves Momma would never know. Mouths watering, visions of cookies and candy filling our heads, our fingers fumbled untying the ribbon. At last it was open! We quickly forgot to be careful, and tore open the box. "Hurry! Hurry! We've got to eat this before we get caught!"

Juddie Cline-Lindley

Alas, instead of cookies and candy, it was cookware! We quickly stuffed it behind the tree and stacked other presents on top thinking we would be secure, our crime undiscovered.

Christmas did bring memorable thoughts and feelings back and I hoped, even with no money, maybe I could still teach my child about tradition, so it was important for me to show him the lights and point out magical things. It was 20 below zero and the gas tank was low; still I bundled my baby up tightly and held him in my arms. As cold as it was I felt warm inside, like I was accomplishing something. That seemed so long ago. Now, I was living in the Arizona desert struggling to survive one day at a time, living in fear that I would never have the opportunity to see my children grow.

One evening, I was sitting in one of the many trailers that I had learned to call home. Suddenly, I felt two sharp pains go down the left side of my face; like someone had taken their fingers and seared them in lightning bolts, drawing on my face. I stood to walk and immediately veered to my left and fell. I struggled to make it to the bathroom unassisted as Bob sat there watching me, offering no help. In the mirror I saw the left half of my face drawn to one side. I looked like a distorted freak. My mind was jumbled and confused and when I tried to speak, I couldn't. I was terrified and as I half stood, half leaned there looking in the mirror, I felt like a trapped animal. All I could think of was getting back to the reservation; my safe haven where people would not make fun of my distorted face.

Bob finally broke away from the TV to see what was wrong. Other than curiosity, since he hadn't hit me this time, I can think of no other reason he checked on me. His response was to tell me to go to the table and he'd get me a cold pop. Confused and dazed I attempted to walk unaided, down the hallway again. I felt like my whole left side was crumpled. I stumbled and fell a number of times before finally reaching the kitchen table. Bob stood there watching, offering no help. By this time the kids had come in the door and I was so "out of it" nothing really mattered to me. They were scared and concerned but Bob brushed them away, telling them it was no big deal.

Bob thrust the pop bottle at me and I attempted to drink out of it but I couldn't get my lips to form. Pop ran down the side of my face onto my clothes. My left eye was large and dilated, and the only thing I remember repeatedly saying was, "my face has fallen." My speech was slurry and incoherent. I was unable to walk without falling. Bob opted to put me in bed in lieu of taking me to the hospital. Had my physical and mental well being been up to par I might have questioned that. It's hard to remember now, but I may have kept my mouth shut fearing if I were to be taken to the hospital questions would be asked. In those days I lived in terror that my "secret" of spousal abuse would be discovered.

Bob kept me in bed for three days, viscously attacking my body as I lay there powerless and helpless to do anything about it. The third evening he finally took me to the emergency room. During these three days of sexual abuse my left eye was paralyzed wide open. The left side of my face was severely drawn to the right, and I was unable to eat or walk without falling. He was the master. He was in control!

I remember the doctor asking me one important question and lying through my teeth as Bob stood there listening. The question: "Have you ever had a head injury?"

My response was, "No, never." Fear for my children's safety was foremost in my mind since Bob was now in complete control. Oh God, what would he do to them if I stayed in the hospital? Though confused, I was able to recall the terrible beating in Farmington; how he kept slamming my head into the cement wall, and the headaches I had for days. I didn't dare tell that secret. I had to protect my children at any cost.

Upon my release from the hospital the road to recovery seemed long and tedious. Julie took over as housekeeper, doing dishes, and grocery shopping. My kids made tremendous sacrifices out of love for me; John, giving up his friends so he could be at my beck and call to comfort and console me, and Julie walking around with a pad in her young hands, making notes of needed can goods. To this day, there is a bond that no one can penetrate or break between the three of us.

Juddie Cline-Lindley

I don't ask anyone to understand this bond. How can they if they haven't been there, lived and experienced it like the three of us?

The doctor gave me cortisone; electric needles penetrated into my face to stimulate the nerves and he taped my eye shut to prevent scar tissue and further damage. The treatments continued after leaving the hospital. Orders were to sit and massage the left side of my face as much as possible for stimulation. There seemed to be some improvement, not much.

As the weeks crept by I was restless and irritated at myself for not healing more quickly. I guess three days of lying in the trailer without medical attention was taking its toll. One evening as I sat rubbing my face, frustration finally took over. I began to cry softly. I clutched at something on the table. It was a piece of the kid's bubble gum. As a child I had never been allowed to chew gum and pop bubbles around Mom. She would cringe and shout how she couldn't stand to hear that noise coming from me. At the next pop she would cross the room and slap me in the mouth. Some things never leave a person, and believe me, Momma's anger and hard slap was something I never forgot.

I wrestled with the idea of chewing some of that disgusting grape bubble gum. It was almost as though I was looking for Momma to cross the room and slap me in the mouth again. Why had this crazy idea or notion come to me? What did this have to do with restoring my face? When I scolded myself with, "Momma's not here," and "What do you have to loose?" The answer became simple. I held that piece of bubble gum in my hand staring at it, for about half an hour. Finally, I unwrapped it and carefully took little nibbles tasting the flavor, telling myself how awful it was. As I look back, I think the thought of chewing the gum was much worse than the act.

I pushed the gum to the left side of my jaw with my finger and gingerly held my face. As the gum became soft and moist I attempted to chew. I soon found myself drooling down my chin. Thank God the kids weren't there to see! They made blowing bubbles look easy, now it was my turn. Trying to force my lips to form so I could blow was a traumatic event in itself. The gum fell out, leaving a disgusting trail of purple juice. I tried over and over again, finally breaking down in tears but determined not to quit.

Day after day I continued my routine of chewing grape bubble gum, not understanding what was driving my dedication. I simply had to do so. I would drool, drop and cry; pick it up and do it all over again. I spent one and a half hours in the morning chewing, and one and a half hours in the evening chewing. I was trained to be regimental, and no matter what, I was going to win this "game" as well. I began to feel more secure in walking and Julie took that as her cue to get me motivated again. One evening she led me by the arm outdoors announcing that it was time for us to jog. Jog! I couldn't even walk without falling! She was determined not to let me go back in the trailer. I would jog and she wouldn't take no for an answer! Finally, I looked at her and said, "Just be there to help me up when I fall."

There were many "falls" in the weeks to come, but as always Julie was there for me.

"Come on mom, you can do it." "Don't give up, we're almost there."

Her pleas turned into commands, reminding me of my childhood and the fierce determination and patience my brother had. There was no way I could let her down, any more than I could have let my brother down. I would prevail; I would win. I no longer allowed myself room for doubt or self-pity. I had children to raise, a husband I was going to divorce, and I WOULD rebuild my life.

I secretly called my brother, John, and told him I didn't know if I would have any "tomorrows." If this inconvenience killed me or, if Bob killed me, would he assume the responsibility of raising my kids?

There was never a hesitation. He answered a very firm, "Yes." "You've got my word, Jude, he'll have to go through me if he's dumb enough to try and get those kids."

I knew exactly what my brother meant, and I knew that once the kids were in his charge, he would kill for them. Peace came over me like warm water from the hot springs in Bisti.

Juddie Cline-Lindley

Now, I could plan my escape.

Bob had been stealing my Indian jewelry and selling it, convinced I was incompetent and unable to know the difference. As part of my plan I continued to let him think that. I began dropping hints that John was at the age where he should be enrolled in karate and I wouldn't mind going myself. Maybe it would help my motor skills if I came clean with the instructor and he would work with me emphasizing use of my left arm and leg.

"After all, Bob, no instructor could possibly be as good as you, but sometimes it's easier to learn the basics from someone else." I appealed to his macho side, telling him he would be the only one qualified to teach us any advanced moves. I could see it working by the expression on his face. I kept telling myself, I could always throw up later. Right now, I had to act believable and sincere to pull this off.

His only comment was, "What will you use for money?"

I replied, "Why, sell some of my Indian jewelry, of course." It worked!

John and I were allowed to attend karate class while Bob sat outside in the car watching our every move through the large plate glass windows. He wasn't about to let me out of his sight and I knew it, so I had to be very careful. We attended six nights a week; the whole time I had the instructor working with me to strengthen my left side.

The jogging, karate and sheer determination began paying off. I was feeling complete and whole again, eager to get on with my life. I began hiding what was left of my Indian jewelry and what few personal possessions I had. Bob had already stolen my son's small TV and sold it along with household items to prolong his tenure in the ranks of the unemployed.

Finally, Bob actually got a job but I was sure this one would be as short lived as the others. I secretly filled out a job application to work for the state prison system; the only requirement being a high school education and no use of elicit drugs. I would definitely be working in a "man's world" but after all I had been through, why not give it a try?

My next move was to tell Bob in private, that I would file for divorce if he ever touched me again. I looked him straight in the eyes and told him death was better than all the years of torment and abuse. NEVER, ever would I go through it again. I warned that if he killed me, my brother John would come after him and take the kids. Bob didn't care about anything I had to say except the part about my brother coming after him. He didn't want to tangle with John.

It had taken me years to get to this point; years to actually confide in my brother and ask for his help in the event of my death. Years of disappointment and lies; unwarranted attacks and abuse. Years of never having a place of my own to call "home," and going to bed with an empty stomach. All these horrible years of pain came back to me. If it cost me my life to make this stand, I was placing my children in God's hands. I prayed asking his forgiveness for giving Him such a heavy burden, when He had so many others. I apologized profusely, assuring the Lord I had no choice, and asked Him to understand. Somehow, I felt better inside; like my prayer was heard and God did understand. That was important to me.

I told Bob I was going to get a job. Immediately the verbal abuse started.

"You just want to get a job so you can find another man," he shouted.

How untrue! I would have been absolutely terrified of finding another animal like him. He hit me in the mouth so hard it sent me spinning. With blood spewing out of my mouth I told him it was over. There, I said it! I had taken my stand and I knew it was going to cost me, physically and emotionally as never before. He tried to drag the kids into it, first by crying, then by threats when they turned deaf ears to his pleas. He told them God was going to strike me dead if I tried to leave and I would go to hell and burn forever. What he didn't realize or care about, was that the kids and I had already been living in hell and the depths of despair, and the only way to look, was up.

Juddie Cline-Lindley

I have been asked what one thing or events finally forced me to get steel in my spine and leave this masochistic and dangerous person. Finally I have come to grips (somewhat reluctantly) with the real truth. It wasn't really just "one thing."

It is true that I was always running and hiding as a child. But it was out of fear for my safety. I was a child hiding from evil that was lurking and waiting to devour me. I was a child running in fear of an adult, with no one to turn to other than my little brother, John. Together we were a team; we could fight these people together. We were as one and remained strong as long as we were together. We were feisty and ornery, and always scheming ways to "get even." Instead of whining and feeling sorry for ourselves, we plotted and made the harsh realities of life a game. As we grew older and went our separate ways, a lot of our strength probably dissipated; or maybe I felt I could no longer turn to my brother for help. After all, I was the big sister.

I made the worst choice of my life when I married Bob, but no one held a gun to my head. I made the decision, regardless of the pressure and circumstances, and I accept full responsibility, having lived with it every day of my adult life.

Being demoralized and brutalized; living in fear of the unknown, could very well have broken a person. My children were the glue that held me together. I had to live and fight back. There was no other choice. When your child looks at you with God-kissed eyes and asks for something reasonable it sometimes becomes hard for a parent to say no. All my children asked for was the chance to live. If I had given up, I shudder to think what would have become of them. They would no longer have known a mother's guidance; shared tears and laughter, secrets and hugs of love. Instead, without a doubt, they would have been subjected to demoralization and pain.

As a youngster, I used to hide in the closet and listen to the old record, "What a Friend We Have In Jesus." Other than my brother, John, this was my only friend. I had no one to turn to or confide in. Sex was a subject that was strictly taboo, and we were never allowed to talk about it. We tried to tell Momma about Boward and Ava, but she dismissed us and became angry, telling us "They didn't mean anything, they were just teasing." Was she really so naïve that she would have sacrificed her own children to abuse? I fear the answer is yes.

The healing process of both body and soul came gradually, not overnight. It took years of mental anguish to reach a decision to leave Bob once and for all. There was no co-dependency, only fear. Fear that if I ever tried to leave this man, God would kill my babies just like my sister and her husband had told me. Some people may laugh at this, but to me, God and my children were my purpose for being. If God became angry with me and turned His back, He could destroy my babies out of retaliation to give me a "wake up call." This message had been drilled into me, to the point that fear blanketed each rational thought. I can't stand to see a little one cry. I may talk tough and walk the walk, but when it comes to kids, anyone's kids, I can't stand to see the pain and hurt look in their little eyes. Tears streaming down innocent little faces just tear me up. Children and the elderly have always been my weakness. My heart longs to care for them any possible way I can.

Living on the reservation was somewhat like reverting back to my childhood and the antics of my brother and me. I fought back at the witcher out of necessity. There was no other place for me to go. I had no family to turn to, and certainly no husband to count on. I was forced to take a stand and fight. That was a good lesson because a healing process had actually begun and I wasn't even aware of it. I had found people who loved me with a genuine child-like love; giving and asking nothing in return. I had found people who needed me, whether they thought I was a medicine woman or just a lost soul wandering in. I was accepted with no questions asked, and I could see and feel their love. Why else in my confused state, after suffering the stroke, my first thought was to retreat to the reservation? Because I knew the Navajo people wouldn't make fun of my distorted face.

Karate also built my self-esteem which had hit rock bottom. It gave me confidence and a self-assuredness and made me begin to feel good about myself. Slowly, body, mind and soul were healing. Even though

Bob kept watching every move, my uneasiness began to fade because I was enjoying myself and learning. I learned about mind control and mental preparedness, keeping my thoughts active and focused. Karate opened a wonderful whole new world to me.

Domestic violence is a horrible thing. Years ago it was not openly talked about as it is today. In today's society, not only is abuse talked about, but also counseling, protection and safe houses are provided for the victims. Children are priorities as well as the battered spouse. There are still narrow-minded individuals who ask, "Why didn't you just leave?" Those people have not walked in my steps, and I earnestly pray they never have to. The very core of my religious convictions had been shaken, but finally, after fourteen years of abuse I knew I had to get out. If this God that I loved and served for so many years felt it necessary to kill my children out of retaliation, then so be it. If I were not going to be alive to protect them, perhaps in His infinite wisdom, death was the answer. I was prepared or I would never have placed that call to my brother. To even think about giving my children away would have been inconceivable, but here I was placing a call to John, asking, no begging, him to raise my kids.

Would I ever endure domestic violence again? Never. Nor should anyone. To be beaten, degraded, threatened and starved is inconceivable to me today. I have regrets just like others who have failed in an endeavor and who have given years of their life struggling with their decision, but are trying to make the best of it and have a semblance of family life. I am pained that I failed, but have peace knowing that it was a union that never should have been.

There are some things in life that we may say we would never do again with profound certainty. Marrying that brutal monster is the one thing I can say would positively never happen. Going to live on the Navajo reservation, on the other hand is an experience I have never regretted. I am privileged. It was there that I found an inner peace and quietness of soul. It was there that I found a true sense of being; acceptance and unconditional love. It was there that I found my family.

I could never have discussed or talked about domestic violence back then, and you have no idea how difficult it is for me to talk about it now. Memories flood back that I had hoped were long forgotten or buried so deep in my mind and soul, that they could never come back and sear my heart again. Writing this book has brought a flood of tears, but through it all, a purging and deep cleansing that I've needed for many years. Now, I can be complete and whole.

Juddie Cline-Lindley

CHAPTER 7

Starting Over: The Healing Path to Recovery

I obtained work at the State Prison as a "guard," as we were called back then. On my application I deliberately left out anything pertaining to medical. I knew, no matter what, I would be able to perform physically, if needed. I had been running a mile and a half nightly, lifting weights and attending karate classes to prepare myself for the academy. My initial interview consisted of a small panel of male officers. When asked if I thought I could protect myself, I answered a resounding, "Yes." The Captain on my hiring board got up and started walking around. He ordered me to stand still, facing the panel, which I did. He proceeded to grab me from behind, placing a choke hold on me. With one sharp thrust I hit him in the groin, doubling him over and breaking his hold. Instead of being angry with me, he had the biggest grin and said, "You're hired!"

I went to work at the men's prison, or the "big house," as it was called, where very few women worked.

Going through the academy was easy for me, even when the drill instructor made me do knuckle pushups in the gravel. I'm sure he was supposed to weed out the women or get us to drop out. He had no idea how strong willed I had become. No matter what, I would do my job and keep my mouth shut. I had kids to feed and I couldn't let them down, or myself.

Upon completion of the academy I was given graveyard shift. I looked at it as though my glass were half full. At least I could get the kids off to school; sleep during the day, and be there for them until bedtime every night. I was sure it could work. I would make it work.

My first night on graveyard the "Yard Man," as he was called, approached me with a scowl on his face. He was skinny with dark hair and probably in his mid 40's. He kind of sauntered as he walked, leaning his head forward like he was such an important man with a tremendous burden on his back. His black boots were spit shined and he carried a heavy metal ring of yard keys hooked on his belt that jangled when he walked. He was a correctional officer as well, but had been there for some time and had the distinction of being somehow above us peons.

I thought he was going to give me a new assignment, instead he gave me a dressing down, telling me I had no business working in a men's prison and that I should be home raising babies. Obviously, he should not have thrust such advice on me. I was no longer this quiet, timid little mouse. I nailed him right back. I knew that if I didn't stand up for myself, these people would eat me alive. I told him how much I would love to be home with my kids, but the only income coming in was mine, and I would feed them at any cost. He snorted and walked away, not liking my response or the fact that a woman slammed him right back.

A few nights later I was relieved from tower duty and told to report to the Yard Office. The Captain wanted to see me. I was a little scared, wondering what I did wrong. I knocked on the door and was told to enter. The Captain and Lieutenant were both there, watching me closely as I walked across the room after shutting the door behind me, as instructed. At first there was small talk; the usual, "how do you like your job," type stuff and the whole time I'm waiting for the hammer to fall; and fall it did. They took turns telling me how much easier things would be if I applied for day shift, leaving me free to party with them at night. I stood there letting all of this sink in, then looked them defiantly in their eyes and said, "Graveyard shift never looked so good."

Juddie Cline-Lindley

I was promptly dismissed and told to return to my assignment. By the next night I had been reassigned to the far tower. During rainy season the dirt lane turned so muddy that mud would sink up over my boots and ooze inside. The normal dry season produced soft, powdery sand that clung to my boots. I had to carry a cloth with me at all times to wipe them off so I could pass surprise inspections. When my meal was delivered, it was always stone cold, but even that didn't matter. I wasn't used to eating very many whole meals anyway.

I would not let them break me.

Things would have gone a whole lot easier if I had given in to sexual requests or dated a ranking officer. But Mom had raised me to have high moral standards; it was embedded and engrained in me. It was part of who I was. I couldn't change. These vulgar, immoral people needed to go home to their own wives and families.

A gal that had just completed the academy was assigned to graveyard shift with me. She was on the heavy side with short dark brown hair and large loose curls. She wore large dark rimmed glasses, smoked heavily and flashed a lot of phony smiles with large white teeth. She made it a point to tell every male officer she encountered that she was a divorced woman. One evening, she called me in my tower and said she wanted to give me some advice. "Sleep with captains and above."

I was very courteous and thanked her then said I would like to give her a little advice: "If you ever want to get anywhere with the Department of Corrections, do it by STANDING on your own two feet."

My advice wasn't well received, and she later went on to marry a major. It has always remained a joke with me. I still think I won.

Bob started sneaking into the trailer while I was working, terrifying and abusing the kids. Julie would sleep on the floor by the door with a ball bat in her hands, always afraid of what he might do next. John was terrified of him but seldom spoke about it. Bob would follow me to work, driving so close to my bumper with his bright lights on, that I was afraid of having an accident. He was very close with the landlord and gained entrance with the pass key on more than one occasion. I always knew when he had been there. I had a shelf of small figurines hanging on the wall. Bob would take the figurines and turn each one around so that they all faced the wall. It always sent a chill up my spine when I walked in and found them. It was his way of letting me know he could get to me any time he wanted.

One afternoon I heard noises coming from the carport. I went to the window and saw Bob with a strange man. They were digging through boxes in the small metal shed. I was irate and immediately asked what they were doing. Bob identified the man as a "preacher" and said they had come to pick up the rest of his things.

"What things?" "You already have everything. What are you doing? I want both of you to leave," I said tersely as I unlocked the door and walked out to the carport.

Instead of sneering or cursing me, Bob smiled sweetly. This was not his normal behavior toward me. I became scared and took quick steps for the door. Bob was right on my heels and entered the trailer before I had a chance to lock the door. He grabbed my arm sinking his nails into it as he twisted my skin. I cried out begging him not to hurt me. The sick smile never left his face as he twisted my skin even harder.

"You can't leave me and break up this family," he said loudly. It was almost as though he was acting for the benefit of others. "I forgive you." He said even louder.

"Forgive me! For what!" I cried out. "Leave me alone. Can't you just go? You're hurting me. My arm is bleeding," I pleaded. He let go of me and acted as though he was crying when he walked out the door.

I knew there had to be a reason for his actions. Why did he bring that "preacher" over knowing he had already taken all of his belongings? Then it dawned on me. When Bob grabbed my arm and put on his theatrical show, it was for the benefit of the man standing outside the open window. Even though the curtain was drawn Bob had to carry on his facade and appear to be a loving husband and father. It was important for him to discredit me. In order for him to do this he would need a witness. A witness that could hear through the open window but not see through the closed drape.

One day while I was napping after working graveyard shift, vicious blows to the base of my head abruptly awakened me. Bob had gained entrance again, and finding me sleeping, straddled me and pounded thrustful blows with his fists to the base of my skull. My screams must have driven him away. I sat and cried for hours over the nightmare revisiting me. Apparently he thought he could drive massive blows to my skull, leaving no bruises on my body. He wanted to make me a vegetable totally dependent upon him.

I finally washed my face. It would soon be time for the kids to come home from school. I went to the kitchen to fix them a snack and found the cupboards bare. He had stolen the food right out of the cupboards! Food that I had worked so hard for, that would feed my precious children. Even with his demented ways, I never really thought he would steal food from babies. My hands were shaking and trembling. My babies had to eat! "Oh God, what can I do?" I pleaded.

The jewelry! Suddenly, I remembered the Indian jewelry that John had been burying in the back yard for me. I dug it up and carefully removed silver dollars from some of the pieces. "There, now I can buy groceries."

That evening was my night off and I heard noises coming from the carport, but John's faithful dog was out there and he never allowed Bob to strike the kids as long as he was around. I always felt comfortable knowing that and encouraged the kids to bring him in when I went to work. I was sure it was Bob again, but having no phone would mean waking the kids up out of a sound sleep to take them to a pay phone with me and report a prowler. So I let them sleep and continued to listen for sounds.

The next morning the dog was dead and the distributor wires had been ripped from my beat up old car. A neighbor boy happened to walk by and see my dilemma. He had one functional arm and was born with a partially deformed arm on the other side. Being handicapped did not stop him. He tackled the car problem like a pro while I removed the dead dog, hoping to spare the kids as much pain as possible. In no time at all the 12-year-old boy had the distributor wires replaced and my car running. God bless him.

Later, I tried to nap since I had to work that night. The kids came in from school shortly thereafter and went outside to play. Suddenly John came running in the door shouting, "Momma, there's a man out there turning off the water!" I jumped out of bed, grabbed my receipt proving the bill had been paid and ran out the back door like a banshee. Yelling at the man, I demanded to know what he was doing, waving my paid receipt like a flag. He looked perplexed. "Your husband called and said you were moving and the water had to be turned off today."

I screeched, "I don't have a husband!"

We both calmed down, and found that Bob had put the utilities in his name when we first moved in, so of course this man was just following orders. As we talked and straightened out this mess, a man from the electric company pulled in. Same story, he was there to turn off the power because we were moving and was instructed that it had to be turned off that day. The gentlemen were nice and we got things sorted out, then I promptly went to the utility companies and had the charges shifted to my name. The temperature was 100 degree plus that day. That's how much feeling Bob had for his own children. He wanted all three of us dead.

The next afternoon, I did something I thought I could never do. I went to a pay phone and called the police. The officer came and was extremely patient. It was like pulling teeth to get any information out of me. I'm sure he could see my embarrassment and shame. Finally, he smiled and said, "Look, I pull over and watch traffic every night in a different location. Tonight I'll park at the front of your street. You're at a dead end aren't you?"

I was thankful that my children would be protected, at least for that night. But it didn't end there. Officer Thompson parked in the same spot night after night, affording the three of us protection and much needed sleep. We became good friends throughout the years, never asking anything of each other and never dating. I shall always be grateful to him.

I'm sure that seeing a police car nearby had its effect on Bob. He never broke into the trailer again. There were several instances away from the house that caused a great deal of concern for our safety, but as long as we were home, there was no more disruption or pain.

Bob often bragged that he would never spend a night in jail. Through the grapevine, I heard that Officer Thompson had arrested him for drunken driving and taken him to jail. While there, he faked a heart attack and spent the night in the hospital. Tests were negative. He was released next day so I imagine he thought he had pulled another fast one to brag about.

It was time for us to move. The floors were rotting out and the couch leg sunk through. There were "soft spots" in the floor of the small kitchen and the lights were blinking from the electrical wiring the landlord put in himself.

The landlord continued to ignore my complaints and I began looking for affordable housing on my meager salary. Bob had signed a year's lease on the trailer and I knew it would not be easy to break the contract. So I resorted to "creative action." I called the fire department and requested a fire safety inspection. When the fireman arrived I explained the safety problem along with the landlord's reluctance to provide maintenance. The fireman wanted to know who did the electrical, and once again I pointed the finger of guilt at the landlord and showed the fireman where he lived across the street. Needless to say, by the time the fire inspector got done with him, the lease agreement was terminated and I immediately rented a small house elsewhere.

The desire to buy my own home seemed to burn within me. I desperately wanted to provide for my children and give them a place they could call home. I wanted them to grow up with stability surrounded by love, without fear for their safety. A home they could be proud of and where their laughter would permeate the walls for years to come.

I noticed a realtors sign and stopped in to speak with the man at the earliest opportunity. I was full of anticipation and excitement when I walked in. In no way was I prepared for the disappointment and ridicule this man dumped on me. He laughed in my face when I told him I had no credit history. He mocked and scorned me for wasting his time, reducing me to tears when I left.

I sobbed my heart out when I got home. I begged God to help me. "Please God, give my kids a home of their own," I pleaded. "Prove that realtor wrong."

Later that week I drove to the bank and asked to speak with the manager. "I'm going to be honest with you," I said. "I'm recently divorced, with very little money and no credit history. But I want to buy my kids a home. What kind of advice can you give me?"

The lady made a few scratches with her pen on a piece of paper and every now and then would say, "mummmm." Finally she looked up at me and said, "Do you own a washing machine?"

"Why no," I said kind of startled by such a strange question.

"Well, I want you to set aside a small amount of money ever payday. When you've saved enough to buy a washing machine go pick one out. Have the bank finance it. I'll freeze the amount it will cost for the washer from your savings. The payments will be automatically deducted. When the washer is paid off, oh say, six months . . . your credit will be established. Then you can save for the house."

I took her advice. The washing machine was paid off and I established credit. More importantly though, I was able to save enough for a down payment and buy my kids a home. We had a telephone and even a new dog for John.

Juddie Cline-Lindley

I still find the pain of that realtor laughing in my face very hurtful. But I did not give up. I had a good cry and got right back up on that horse and showed him who was boss.

At work I was able to deal with the sexual harassment. I had to because I needed the job. To this day I absolutely hate it if someone whistles at me, even in jest. One time when crossing the prison yard, a big burly guard came up to me and said, "Just stand behind me. I'll protect you and not let anyone hurt you." I hated that! It wasn't concern speaking, but the macho side of this phony. I swore that someday jerks like him would eat those very words.

I began asking about joining the prison SWAT team. It paid an extra sixty dollars per month hazardous duty pay and that would help on the grocery bill. I was shot down cold by a captain who replied, "We don't let cunts on the SWAT team." I resolved to someday prove him wrong. Someday I would be a SWAT team member. It took me five years but I finally got there. I received my hazardous duty pay and helped pay the grocery bill. But more importantly, I proved something to that poor excuse for a human being.

I had been attending college classes at correctional expense. I felt that I would be foolish to turn down free education and training, so I talked it over with the kids and the three of us decided to make even more sacrifices in order for me to do this. I loved to study anything that pertained to criminal justice and excelled in the classes. Police officers in these classes often teased me about being the teacher's pet and always asking what grade I received on a test. What they didn't know, nor did I ever tell them, was that the instructor was the attorney who handled my divorce, and if he ever wanted to flunk anyone, it would have been me.

I had been in the attorney's office going over last minute paperwork on my divorce when he asked me if I wanted to leave for a while and go for a ride. He said he wanted to show me his new horse. Of course, naïve and gullible that I was, I said sure. When we got to his place he insisted on showing me the inside of his house, and pointing down the hallway, he said there was a special room I might be interested in. I felt a lump rise in my throat; then anger. I told him I thought his horse would be more interesting. Boy, did I ever deflate his ego! He couldn't wait to get me back to his office, and not another word was ever said. When I signed up for college classes and saw his name as one of the instructors, I thought, "Oh well!" But it didn't deter me one bit.

Working and studying hard, I was determined to fill out an application for an Internal Affairs Investigator. A trainee position had become available, and I wanted to learn so badly. I knew my chances of getting it were next to none. After all, I was a female working in a men's institution and there had never been a female investigator before. "What the heck," I thought. I'll give it my best shot. An all male panel of investigators interviewed me. A few days later I was called in. The position was mine.

My new supervisor made it quite clear to me that he "went out on a limb" for me, and he was the deciding factor in the final choice. I felt honored but I also knew I would work hard and was a fast learner. With just a little patience, in time he would know that he had made the right selection. Max appeared very kind, often talking about his wife and five children. He was a short bald headed man of slender build who wore a false bridge in his mouth and tinted prescription glasses. He didn't have a loud booming voice and would have to raise it to be heard over the other investigators at staff meetings. The others often joked out loud about him, but he was not one to laugh at himself, retreating to his office and shutting the door when he felt it was beginning to get too personal. All the while, I was beginning to feel relaxed and content, settling into my new position with ease. I learned to investigate homicides, accidents, drug smuggling and assaults to name a few. The whole time I kept telling myself, "I'm learning. This is great."

Gradually, Max began calling me at home on specific cases. I certainly didn't mind him calling, after all it was work related, but I just couldn't shake a sinking feeling. The calls increased. Then he began showing up on my doorstep unannounced. His behavior was crossing the boundary line of concern for a fellow officer and I was fighting mad. He insisted that we had to have lunch together everyday, and I was extremely embarrassed over his attention in front of the other investigators. It was easy to read them and I felt sure they thought I had something going with this guy.

By this time, Max was calling me at home telling me he was sure he loved me. Unable to stand much more, one day I asked the lead investigator to go for coffee with me. We sat down and I laid it on the line, telling him there wasn't anything sexual going on between Max and myself, but that he absolutely would not leave me alone. All I wanted was to be left alone so I could do my job and told him so. The lead investigator thanked me for being so candid and admitted that the other investigators all felt there was more than a working relationship between Max and me as well.

Max's behavior escalated the more I resisted his advances. Finally, he made every deliberate attempt to let it spill over in the work place. He would call me in for documented sessions (his documentation) about my "attitude" in the work place, making for a hostile work environment. He would ask cold-blooded killers if I was polite and courteous enough when I interviewed them (I taped everything.) The pressure and sexual harassment became more than I could bear. Actually, it was probably the embarrassment and shame of the thought that others were convinced I was having an illicit relationship with Max.

Word had filtered into our office via a prison snitch that a drug shipment was about to be smuggled in. The drugs were going to be left hidden in a certain location one night and were to be picked up the following day by inmates allowed to work outside the walls. All of the investigators in the office had to hide on their bellies, armed and playing soldier on the specified date and wait most of the night for the occurrence. They were armed and waiting with the exception of me. Just before the bust, Max called me in for another one of his documented sessions. He said the reason I wasn't allowed to go was because if one of the suspects fired on me he was sure I would shoot to kill, not wound. He wrote it up and put it in my file.

I've always found it amusing and considered it a "badge of honor" if you will. Maybe this was the one time Max was right about me.

Feeling that I could take no more, I went to the Major, who was the next step up and head of all the Internal Affairs Departments for the state prisons. I told him what was happening and that I just wanted to be left alone to do my job. He admitted that he also thought Max and I had a relationship and by his attitude I could tell he didn't think there was anything to complain about. It was just something I should live with and keep my mouth shut about. Finally, he said that Max replaced the old Supervisor of Internal Affairs because of a big blow up that had to do with sexual harassment, and he wasn't about to let the same thing happen twice. "We don't want to wash our dirty linen in public!" he declared. "Therefore, you will be transferred."

I was shocked! I was being penalized for not sleeping with Max and told the Major so. He didn't see it my way, and felt that transferring me and covering it up would be best for all. Several years later I heard that Max had lost his position, transferred to another prison, and was being sued for sexual harassment. Pending a resolution, he had been reassigned and reduced to working in the prison mailroom.

Upon transferring to another prison, I requested Aikido self defense training when it became available. My request was processed and approved and upon completion of the training, the department made me the self-defense instructor for five institutions.

A macho guard in a class I was teaching thought there was only one purpose for women. One day I made an example out of him by saying in front of everyone that when we crossed the prison yard he wouldn't have to worry about a thing. He could stand behind me and I'd protect him. That zing made him eat humble pie and we became friends after that.

I've never thought that I was pretty or desired by men. It's just that when working with mostly male officers, many with no morals or scruples, life became a game for them, another notch on the belt, if you will. Sexual harassment was rampant in the system. If the few women that did hold a position as "guards" couldn't handle the heat, we were told to get and go back to being housewives.

Juddie Cline-Lindley

The state prison selected twelve of us state wide to attend the peace officer academy. Oh well, what was another academy, I thought. I attended, and enjoyed it. Later, at the urging of a supervisor on the psychiatric unit, I interviewed for a counseling position and attained it. They assigned me to work with violent male inmates, the worst of the worst. The extremely violent, psychotic ones were moved to one location, my unit. I thought it couldn't be any worse than what I had already been through and convinced myself it would be easy for me. Instead it was a tremendous challenge with few rewards. We always had to be very careful and watch each other's backs. Without warning we could be attacked at any moment and severely injured by these individuals. Life was never dull!

I received word from the training officer that in order to keep my peace officer status current I would have to attend some training. The training, as it turned out, could last a week with me having to attend in another city. Absolutely no way was I going to leave my daughter (a teenager by this time) for a full week! P A R T Y TIME! I immediately began asking where I could obtain this training without going out of town and was given a state highway patrol officer's name and telephone number by another employee. The officer was the training officer for the Department of Public Safety. I called him. He agreed one hundred percent with my assessment of teenagers and extracurricular activity, and agreed to come to the prison and give me the needed updated training.

John had just joined the Navy, and the pride I had for this boy swelled within me. I remember him walking in the door one afternoon and as my back was turned very quietly he said, "I just joined the Navy. I ship out in three days." I knew he had to wait until my back was turned to make his announcement. He wouldn't be able to stand the pained look on my face. I held him and cried. My son was indeed a man standing tall.

The police training officer and I had communicated over my updated training and he set the time and date at his earliest convenience. He was to meet me in the prison lobby after I clocked out and we would go over my training needs. He never showed. I wasn't happy waiting in that lobby an hour for a man that didn't appear, especially when he was the one who chose the time and date. Besides, now I was going to have to fight that horrible rush hour traffic trying to get home! Later I found out an officer had been injured in a training accident and he was called away on emergency.

Eventually we connected and I led him back to the psychiatric unit advising him to "watch his back." Some of the big burly patients lined up in the doorway and hallways checking him out. Finally, one of the violent offenders that closely resembled the genie that comes out of the bottle (except this genie was covered in tattoos) became convinced he knew the officer. He kept calling him, Joe. I knew who the inmate was talking about and "Joe" was one kick butt karate dude. I had noticed the resemblance immediately when I first met the officer, and figured as long as the inmates thought that he was "Joe," his safety would not be an issue. It never was, but I later found out the officer could have handled it anyway.

The officer and I became fast friends and lovers. A mutual respect for each other and a caring for the patients sealed our bond. We literally spent hundreds of hours of our own time devising lesson plans on Ki breathing, exercises and special needs planning for these violent individuals. Everything had to be approved by the head psychiatrist prior to being taught, but the results were phenomenal. Our group started with 14 violent individuals, some falling off their chairs due to the heavy medication needed to control them. Each course or level lasted six weeks. Prior to our Ki/Kiatsu classes it had not been uncommon to have two or three "codes" called a day. A "code" is called when a fight erupts either between inmates or inmates attacking staff, and all 14 of our bad boys had been involved in numerous codes.

We taught the patients Ki breathing to help them relax, and unify as a group to help each other. Whenever one was having a "bad day" (his behavior was escalating and he was ready to go off) he would knock on cell doors and tell the others in the group that he was having problems. I would often find the head psychiatrist standing in the hallway watching them through the window, shaking his head in disbelief. At the completion of the six-week course all 14 graduated, attending every class. All 14 had been put on reduced medication that controlled their violence, and there had not been a single code called on any of the 14 the entire six weeks. The classes were a success, but more importantly, they gave these men a purpose for being, and for some it was probably the first time in their lives they actually cared about others.

I increasingly found myself looking at the Navajo rug Kee's aunt had made for me. I ran my fingers along the embedded grains of sand and stroked Grandmother's old jewelry. It was like I was still running inside but knew I could never escape the feeling of love and devotion I carried with me for the Navajo people. Sadness and yearning to return to the reservation finally won out.

My love and I discussed commitment and decided to each request transfers to a northern location where there would be a prison for me to work at and a new assignment for him with the state police. Julie was a senior in high school and only had one semester left to graduate when our transfers came through. Like the trouper she has always been, she packed her bags, leaving her friends and school behind to make the move with us. She completed her last semester at another high school with barely a complaint and began taking classes at the junior college. John would come home on leave every chance he got, and was so relieved that there was a man in my life. His only comment was, "Good, now I won't have to worry as much." When I married, I could see a kind of peace settle over John.

One day I received an unusual phone call from John. He said, "Mom, it's so strange. A dark cloud has covered the ship for a number of days. Several of my buddies and I asked about it and were told it was smoke from a factory on shore." He went on to say he made trip(s) to sick bay. John was not one to complain, so I knew there was a concern there. A knot tightened in my stomach and I tried to dismiss it as a mother's concern for her son serving his country in the Mideast during perilous times.

Living in the northern part of the state would bring an occasional Indian to our door, selling things. One night a man, who called himself Owen, brought a beautiful framed painting and wanted $20 for it, saying he just needed gas money to get home. I gave him the $20 but I had restless sleep for the next two nights. There was an unusual feeling I had about this man. Something I don't know how to explain. But I was convinced he was someone special. Eventually my suspicions proved true as he returned many times. We became good friends; his family became our family, spending holidays and special events together and Owen's wife, Mary, became my sister. As sisters we sometimes argue and have our differences. Mary has an ornery streak and I have to be on my toes at all times, so she doesn't get one up on me. Still, she's very loving, with child like qualities.

I also become acquainted with Navajo Medicine Man, Benny Singer. Soon, Benny became more than just my friend; he became Uncle Benny and someone I loved and trusted. Over the years Uncle Benny has always been there for me, and has allowed me to attend ceremonies in Prayer Hogans that many Navajo are not allowed in, let alone Anglos. Sometimes we speak in Navajo, sometimes in English; other times he just looks deep into my eyes and reads my heart with neither of us speaking a word. Uncle Benny has no phone and lives off the beaten track on old bumpy reservation roads, but out of the clear blue, when one of the kids are sick, he'll knock on the door with a prayer bundle in his hand and asks, "Who needs me?"

I don't question his uncanny ability to "know things." I accept, which is Navajo way. Uncle Benny has always been very patient with me. He usually takes the time to explain in great detail any questions I may have about specific ceremonies, the Navajo people, the healing with herbs, or his sacred prayers. He has no problem telling me if it's not time to reveal something to me, so I'll accept his answer; store it in my mind until later and bombard him with questions another time. He knows me well, and he knows I won't quit asking until I have an answer. There is a deep, unconditional love and acceptance between us, and Uncle Benny officiated the ceremony when I was accepted into the Salt born for the Tobacco Clans.

Juddie Cline-Lindley

Benny Singer

My uncle is unsure of his real age, having been born in a hogan he can only safely guess. He walks with a spring in his step and a twinkle in his eye when he kids me. Other days he takes slow, deliberate steps and his serious side comes out. When he does three and five day prayers for people, he wears his ceremonial jewelry and my what a display! Large turquoise and silver bracelets, belt buckle with numerous turquoise stones, bolo tie and long turquoise traditional necklace. Sometimes he wears a folded scarf tied to his head. Other times I see his wide smile as he approaches me with his western hat and silver concho hat band I gave him. It's traditional for medicine men to dress this way and I stand back and marvel every time I see it. His face is weather worn and his cheeks still turn rosy with obvious blush despite his brown tone skin when I tease him. His smile can light a room as he lowers his head in laughter and says, "Juddie, Juddie" over and over again in broken English.

My clan or family brother, Owen Jr., was getting married traditionally in a hogan with Uncle Benny officiating. He had used the traditional barter system for his first two wives, trading cows and sheep to their families for them, but with this marriage there would be no trading. He was marrying a white woman and the mother of his child. I was granted permission to video tape the ceremony and turned off the camera at the completion of it. Uncle Benny's ornery nature began to surface and I could see him looking my way and smiling. I wasn't sure what he was up to, but he was a great one for playing jokes, and usually it was on me. Suddenly, he stood and announced that I was not to leave the hogan until he had found me a husband. I knew I had to think quickly since he was revered and looked up to by the tribe. The others may not know that he was kidding. I sprang to my feet and addressed him as well as the others, blurting out that I didn't have enough cows and sheep to buy a husband. Uncle Benny laughed loudly. So did the crowd and my virtue was saved. Later, I chuckled at his practical joke but also gave a sigh of relief. Many Navajo had no idea he was a jokester, having only seen his serious side. What if he hadn't started laughing?

Juddie Cline-Lindley

Over time, numerous Navajo would come to our door. If hungry they were always fed; if thirsty they were given something to drink. I would save clothing and old tires, distributing them out of the kitchen or back yard. Having lived on the reservation, I knew an old tire that would still hold air might just get one of my people back home. I love to barter with these people so when my husband complained about the front door being too heavy and made the mistake of telling me he wanted to get rid of it, I obliged him. He came home a few days later and it was gone. I had traded it to a Navajo woman who said it was just what she was looking for. The same thing happened with the washer and dryer and the doghouse we no longer needed. That's when he put his tools under lock and key.

My husband didn't always understand Navajo way and was tolerant at best. He had heard me talk of the Navajo but had never really seen me with them, so it was a different situation for him to grow accustomed to. One day he returned home from work, in uniform, to find the entire living room filled with Navajo; standing room only. He looked puzzled and asked what was going on. I replied that the Navajo were upset with the unfair treatment they were receiving from the police department so I was organizing them for a protest march. Furious and fearing retribution and embarrassment from fellow officers, he threw his arms in the air, shouting, "I'm out of here!" as he stormed out the door. There was a silence that lasted maybe 30 seconds, then the room filled with giggles from the women. Try as he might, he never fit in, nor understood these beautiful people. His lack of patience used to irritate me, but I knew this white boy from California was very uncomfortable in their presence.

I was acquainted with a couple that tried my patience on many occasions. Had it not been for love, acceptance and toleration, we would all have hated each other long ago. William is "rough looking" to say the least. He is slender, with medium build; and when sober, very conscious about his appearance. He plays and sings in an all Indian country western band and I never could quite figure out how he is able to accomplish this feat, especially when his voice is slurry from cheap liquor. In that state he has a hard time managing to stand and walk as he swaggers down the street.

William had been a very well known artist in the 60's until alcohol got the best of him, and in the 90's, made a comeback, just as good or better than before. William sports a scar across his throat from a vicious knife attack outside an Indian bar. To hear William tell it, "This crazy Indian was jealous because I could sing better than him. So he hid outside the bar behind a truck and jumped out and tried to cut that voice box thing out of my neck." William survived and so did his voice box, so he continued singing at the same country bar.

Even facing travesty and travails, William's sense of humor is usually intact. I have fed William and Martha on many occasions and always have hot coffee in the winter and a cool drink (tea or water) for them in the summer, as they are usually "on foot" and hitching rides.

Martha is short and round, with beautiful long, black hair reaching to her buttocks. She comfortably fits under William's armpit, and he forever complains to me (in her presence) about her weight gain "from eating too much fry bread." Together, they live in a hogan in Sheep Springs, a remote area on the Navajo reservation, and care for their horses, coming to town on a whim or when William has to perform. As often as William complains about Martha, there is an undisguised love between the two of them, and they are almost always inseparable. They like to "tattle" on one another, and I, acting like a stern mother reprimand the perpetrator, much to the satisfaction and delight of the "teller."

William got into another fight, and this time had his scalp cut severely with a broken beer bottle. He was transported to the Indian hospital where metal sutures were put in his head and he was released. About a week later he and Martha came to see me, with William complaining incessantly about a headache, which is highly unusual for William, or any Navajo for that matter.

This time it was Martha's turn to tattle on William. "William's not being very nice to me. He yells at me. Tell him to stop. Tell him how lucky he is to have me."

"Shame on you William," I scolded. "I don't want you picking on Martha anymore. You ARE lucky to have her. Look how long you've been together. No one else would've stayed this long. She loves you, and you better treat her right."

Then turning to Martha I jokingly said, "Now hon, if he keeps treating you badly, you just take a pair of pliers when he's sleeping and pull those staples out of his head. He'll be real careful how he treats you after that."

Martha nodded in agreement, sober faced, as William shouted, "Don't give her any ideas. She might get crazy on me!" His sudden response caused us both to laugh loudly.

The next day Martha stood outside the door as William distanced himself, wearing a ball cap. Unusual behavior for William, I thought. I had never seen him wear a baseball cap before, and questioned (to myself of course) just why William was standing away from the doorway with his back turned to me.

"William's mad at me again," Martha complained. "He was being mean to me again last night and I just did what you told me to do."

"Martha, what did I tell you to do? What are you talking about?" Then I remembered what I had jokingly said about the pliers. "Oh my God, Martha! Did you hurt William's head?"

Just then William turned around to face me and took a few hesitant steps toward me, almost as though he were scared. "William, come here," I demanded. "Let me look at your head. What did Martha do to you? Are you OK? What are you wearing that hat for?"

William mumbled something about Martha being a crazy Indian and how all women were crazy, as he looked at the ground, still hesitant to face me.

"William, take off your hat," I said softly, trying to use a different approach. He reminded me of a little kid with chocolate all over his mouth whose momma would ask, "Did you sneak into the candy?"

William came closer and took off his hat. As Martha stood passively by, William turned around to show me the back of his head, and then asked for a couple of aspirins.

I was horrified! One side of the metal suture was sticking straight out and the other end was firmly planted in his head. "My God, what happened here!" I exclaimed.

"This crazy Indian just took your advice," William said. "We were sitting on the couch watching TV. She patted her lap, and told me to come lay my head on her. I thought she was getting one of those notions. You know what kind I mean."

"Yes, William, I think I do. You thought she was trying to get sweet on you. Right?"

He nodded his head in agreement. With shaky voice he continued. "I moved over to her and laid my head on her lap. Then all of a sudden she whipped out a pair of pointy nosed pliers and grabbed one of my staples and wouldn't let go! It hurt bad. I'm wearing the hat to protect my head. As long as I wear the hat, it reminds me I have a staple sticking out of my head, so that I don't forget and comb my hair. That would really hurt."

"Shame on both of you," I said. "I don't want anymore fussing. I want you both to behave. Martha, you're lucky to have William love you as much as he does. William, you're lucky to have Martha. No other Indian woman would put up with you for as many years as she has. Now, both of you go straight to the hospital and get his head fixed. Do you understand?"

Both stood with heads lowered, as "Momma" chewed them out, then they left together in good spirits to get William's head fixed. Next day William was no longer wearing his ball cap.

I was very careful about giving advice and joking with them after that incident. I never, ever thought Martha took me seriously when I told her to use the pliers on poor William's head. Even William laughed with me when I jokingly suggested it, so I don't think he really thought she would do it either.

They're still very much a couple and deeply committed to one another. One thing is different, though. William walks softly and no longer calls Martha "a crazy Indian," reserving that statement for his Native American adversaries at the country western bar.

Time passed and I didn't see or hear from William and Martha. I grew concerned. After all, these were my children, too. It's not unusual for the earth to swallow up a Navajo, and they resurface when they choose, so I continued to worry silently, still not feeling right about it. They were usually at my door long before this snitching each other off.

Several months passed and suddenly I looked up and they were both standing before me. This time William spoke, asking for food and water while little Martha stood in the background with head lowered. This was not right and I knew it.

"Martha, honey what's wrong?" "You've been gone a long time. Has William been treating you alright?"

She remained silent and still did not look up. I walked toward her sensing a terrible loss or dread. Something bad had happened and I knew it. As I stepped closer I saw her bruised and battered face. Her eye sockets looked sunken, the whites of her eyes almost a blood color.

"Martha," I said softly. "Tell me what happened." She glanced toward William as if pleading for strength and him to speak the words for her. He stepped forward and in low tones said, "Come over here, and I'll tell you what happened. Martha can't talk about it, yet."

He and Martha had been in Farmington and took a short cut back to where they were staying, late one night. They passed by the railroad tracks and were attacked by four young men. It was gang initiation, and Martha was the prey. William broke down as he spoke of the struggle to aid her and showed me the stitches from the broken beer bottle they used on him. Martha was savagely beat beyond recognition and gang raped. She had just been out of the hospital a short time. Now, the detectives in Farmington wanted them both to testify against their assailants. William was ready, but he worried it would be too much on Martha and wanted me to talk to her.

I held her in my arms and told her how brave she and William had been. I expected nothing less, for they were Navajo. Now, she must go one more step.

"Put these bad men away, Martha." "Be strong, honey. Both of you be strong. Know that I love you and I am so proud of you."

"Martha, I am proud of you because you used the inner strength of a Navajo and refused to die."

"William, I am proud of you because you fought back with all your might for the woman you love."

"Have you two been through any ceremonies to take the bad dreams away?" "I will burn cedar and say prayers for you tonight."

They were consoled and wanted to make sure "momma" knew how hard they fought. I hugged them both and cried openly with them, sharing their pain. Later, they were fed and when they stepped back out into the sunshine, their beautiful child like smiles were once again on their faces and Martha looked up at me, giving me one last hug before departing on foot.

I heard through the Navajo grape vine, William and Martha's testimony sent the bad guys to prison for a very long time.

A Navajo friend was reminiscing about his family and late grandfather to me. I, having the distinction and privilege of being his granddaughter's godmother, always welcomed "Big Bear" into our home. I enjoyed listening to him chuckle as he told stories he had seen or witnessed with the Navajo, or even perhaps read and changed a few facts around to make the stories his own.

"Big Bear," as I often called him, was a large Navajo man in his mid to late 50's. His skin was brown and he had wide, full cheeks. Broad shouldered and seemingly shy; in a glance there could be no mistake in guessing that he would present a handful if provoked to anger. All 280 pounds of solid mass could destroy an adversary with one thrust of his massive fist.

But when Big Bear talked of his family and grandchildren, a softness and glow settled over him. Suddenly, he was like a tamed mountain lion. Wanting nothing but the best for his family, he encouraged his children to pursue an education. He drove his daughter to school daily rather than wait for the bus that often ran late. Punctuality and education were important to him and he instilled that in each one of his children. "Get an education. Make yourself proud. Make me proud. And make your people proud," I often heard him say to them.

One day as Big Bear was reminiscing, he began to chuckle and told me about a movie that had been filmed at Pinedale, Church Rock and Iyanbito years ago. Several hundred Navajo had been hired as extras. Their job was to come swooping down on horseback, whooping and hollering attacking the whites.

One Navajo in particular had been singled out to translate the instructions of the director to the other Indians. A scene called for a rifle to be fired and a Navajo was to fall from his horse, acting as though he were shot. The director thought he had made this clear when he told his Navajo translator to pick one of the Indians and instruct him to fall when the shot rang out.

Instead, the translator became confused and instructed *all* the Navajo to fall from their mounts when the single rifle shot was fired. The director was not happy to see several hundred Navajo felled by a single round!

Eventually, things began running more smoothly. A scene called for a solider to get buried in sand up to his neck by the marauding savages. The man's body was placed in a wooden crate for protection and lowered into the ground with only his head and neck visible. Honey was poured over his head and ants were strategically placed nearby.

The scene was filmed without a problem and the film crew left the area. The director instructed one of the Navajo to dig up the solider, and then drove away. It seems the Navajo left behind with the task of digging, became distracted. He left the area shortly after the others, "forgetting" his assignment. Later, being reminded, he hurried back to the area and uncovered the solider. An ant-eaten actor said some very ugly things to his Indian rescuer!

Iyanbito, where much of the movie was filmed, is also known as Pera to the older Indians. Translated, Iyanbito means "Buffalo Springs." It's a beautiful mountainous area well known to the Native Americans and perfect for filming a western movie.

A Navajo man was hitch hiking in the area when an older white couple felt compassion and stopped to give him a lift. Unknown to them, the Navajo had a speech problem along with mental malfunction. The Anglo gentleman asked the Navajo where he was headed. "Maybe my wife and I can take you there," he offered.

The confused Navajo, tried to pronounce the word Pera, (which sounds like Purr-e-a.) Instead of pronouncing the letter "p" he added a "k" and a few other letters as well.

Later, the Navajo was talking to a friend of his telling about the peculiar behavior of the Anglos. "They drove away real fast," he said. "As soon as I told them where I wanted to go."

His friend gave him a quizzical look and asked, "Where did you tell them you were going?"

"Why, I said I wanted a ride to Korea," was the reply.

Early one morning, there came a tap, tap, tap at the door. I was sleepy eyed with hair hanging down in my face, as I slowly opened the door a crack. "Good morning princess!" came a cheery voice on the other side.

"Go away, I don't want to buy anything today. It's Sunday and it's 7:30," I growled. "Come back some other day," having recognized the young male voice, and shutting the door.

Tap, tap, tap it went again, sounding like a woodpecker. I opened the door fully thinking my sleepy appearance and ugly demeanor would scare him away. Instead he spoke like a little chirping bird with a big smile on his face, "Are we having a bad day today princess?" This time I slammed the door in his face!

The third time, tap, tap, tap again. I threw open the door and yelled, "Just what in the heck do you want!" This time I was wide-awake and there was no mistaking my anger as I glared at the young man who was causing my early morning intrusion. We both started laughing hysterically at the same time. I invited him in and bought some Kachinas from him; fed him and sent him on his way.

Word began filtering to me from the many Navajo that visited my home that so and so said they knew me. I was the white woman that lived on the reservation years ago. As time went by, more Navajo told me this and it became very heart wrenching for me. I had walked away and never looked back because of the pain of leaving. Now it was as though these people were forcing me to face it. Why now, after all of these years?

One day, an elderly Navajo woman came to my door and I invited her inside. She studied my face carefully and finally smiled. She said, "You're the white woman that used to live on the reservation. I know about you. There was a peyote meeting going on one time, and when the peyote was passed to you, you jumped up and ran out. Oh yes, we all know about you!"

She was right! I couldn't run and hide any longer. Oh God, what had happened to Kee? What happened to Grandmother and Grandfather, Kerry Chee, Albert and Suzie?

My new informative friend became my Navajo mother. She said that the people had been told that the children and I were dead and had gone into mourning for us. She didn't need to say more. I knew Bob told them that vicious lie, purposely hoping to close the door behind me. It didn't matter. I couldn't look back anyway.

Uncle Benny was allowing me to bring people to the prayer hogan. As time went on we formed an even deeper bond and respect for one another. He knows my heart and the love I have within me for his people, and has always respected my wishes. He patiently began teaching me prayers and showing secret things to me in his old battered suitcase where he carries his prayer feathers, corn pollen, and other sacred objects. Why, I wondered, was he showing these secret things to me and not to one of his own people? I felt honored at his trust in me.

Years of sexual harassment in the prison system had taken its toll. Years of keeping this garbage inside of me was giving me headaches and loss of appetite. I now had a husband who said there was no need for me to ever receive this type of treatment again and insisted I fight back. I went to a psychologist, Dr. Larry Stevens, and literally poured my heart out. He was compassionate, caring and immediately felt like a friend I could trust and confide in. When I retired from the prison system a huge burden lifted, and I resolved to never allow anyone to treat me like a sub human again. I have no problem advising anyone to seek professional help when the burden becomes too heavy, and have referred a number of correctional employees and police officers to Dr. Stevens for treatment. I did myself, as well as my family a tremendous service by seeing him. I retired and a huge burden of pain and bitterness was lifted.

CHAPTER 8

FULL CIRCLE

With retirement behind me it was now time for me to heal, both body and soul. Being a workaholic for so many years and working two jobs many times, left me feeling like I had too much time on my hands and besides, I needed another challenge. I went back to college, but still needed something more. I wanted to do full time police work and leave the counseling to the pros. I needed to give myself the extra, "push" to make the competitive side come out in me once again. Mission accomplished.

I filled out an application with the sheriff's department, passed the test and polygraph, and was accepted to start in the police academy. Physically, I knew there would be no problem. I easily ran the required distance, lifted weights and mentally prepared myself for this particular challenge. The stigma of "old age" wasn't a problem for me either. You're as old as you feel. Get past any head trips and get on with your life. By the time I completed the academy, I was class leader with high academic scores; and scored extremely high with weapons and self-defense (must have been all the practice I had shooting the chickens in the butt and defending myself when I was a kid.) More importantly to me, I scored first place in physical fitness, beating out kids in their early 20's.

There were a number of Native Americans in the academy, both Navajo and Apache. I immediately felt at ease and our friendship blossomed from day one. I often kidded the Apaches, telling them that Kee Benally had drilled into my head to "stay away from them Apaches. Them mean people." We laughed about Kee's words, but the red flags were still up. The academy director acted like he disliked Native Americans and it was obvious to them as well as myself. Sometimes they would take longer to answer a question, or extra time would be spent on a test, not because they were mentally slow, but because they had to decipher the English that was spoken to them, changing it from Apache or Navajo then back to English. Then they could answer the question or complete the test, but sometimes it just took a little longer. I knew this was happening and did my best to help them in any way that I could. The director's job was to weed out people that he felt were undesirable. It always amazed me how he felt that qualified, competent individuals who spoke two languages were undesirable.

Hank was a middle aged Apache who had been a police officer for many years on the White Mountain Apache Reservation and appeared to be the spokesperson for the group of Apaches in the class. Even though they were already commissioned tribal officers, the tribe sent them to an Anglo academy to learn the laws so they could become cross-commissioned and arrest Anglos, as well as Apaches. Hank wasn't a green, new recruit; but a seasoned officer with many years of experience under his belt, and undoubtedly was amused by some of the younger cadets in the class. As the Apaches were slowly eliminated or "kicked out," if you will, I could see a look of anger and stubbornness cross Hank's face. Hank had been involved in the AIM (American Indian Movement) and had borne arms to protect the Apache's water rights. I knew he was not one to fool with.

One day, an Apache too many had been eliminated and Hank was black with anger. At lunchtime the Apaches gathered around Hank's truck as he said over and over again, "That piece of crap." His reference was to the academy director. The other Apaches were in one accord. I agreed with them, but my experience of being able to think and understand Indians as well as whites, was always something I could use to advantage. I had been treated by the Apaches as one of them from the beginning. They knew I wouldn't lie to them and respected what I had to say, so I devised a plan and laid it out.

"Karrice, come here. Your dad's a captain with the tribal police department and the director treats you better than the rest. He wants to suck up to your dad. That makes you the key. After lunch you go to him and tell him if any more Apaches go; you go. Do you understand? Can you do it?"

Karrice answered affirmably and did as she was told while the others anxiously watched. No more Apaches were eliminated after that. Later, I learned Hank always carried a thousand rounds of ammo in his tribal truck with various weapons. I was told Apaches always come prepared.

Going through the policy academy required numerous testing. Besides the written testing, there were firearms, driving, and self-defense to name a few. One of the cadets was a former fire captain from Los Angeles who decided to make a career change. He was slender with short reddish hair, always cracking jokes and looking forward to the end of the day so he could sneak a drink. He was careful and bragged about his motto to some, "Work hard, play hard." "The Fireman," was his nickname.

The Apaches especially got a kick out of him and we "allowed" him in our "special group" to a small extent. He made us laugh. He wasn't a snitch. In short, he bugged to the middle and kept his mouth shut. His significant other was convinced she had been an Indian in her past life and "The Fireman" believed her, or at least said he did. I often told the Indians to humor him when he talked of this. He meant well. Besides, before it was all over they may need an ally. So they listened and continued to be entertained throughout the academy.

The defensive driving course was on the agenda and we looked forward to hammering our foot to the metal. The academy director teamed us up with a partner for several days of driving. Mine was none other than "The Fireman." I felt light and giddy, like butterflies were floating around in my stomach as the cars roared through the obstacle course, weaving in and out of the rubber cones that are used for road construction detours.

We were being watched closely and evaluated on our performance. All of us were under stress and told constantly by the director that his job was to weed out the "bad apples" and get rid of the undesirables. At this point in the academy, we had worked hard to get this far and none of us wanted to get kicked out because of failure. I'm sure we created even more stress on ourselves as we buckled up and floored the vehicles while the Director stood there holding a stopwatch. We were told to increase our speed with each turn and the pressure was on.

I felt like my nerves were frying as I hit some cones, knowing points would be docked from my score.

"Darn it!" I shouted. "What in the heck is the matter with you?" I yelled out loud to myself.

"The Fireman" leaned back acting relaxed with a Cheshire grin on his face.

"Deep and wide," he said.

"What in the heck are you talking about," I snapped. "I'm screwing up and all you can say is "Deep and wide." "Are you nuts?"

Then "The Fireman" spoke some very profound words explaining himself as I roared through the obstacle course.

"Just think of sex when you make your turns. Deep and wide. Deep and wide," he continued repeating in a slow, monotone voice reminiscent of a person with a hang over.

Suddenly I laughed. The obstacle course became so easy. It was fun! I glanced over at "The Fireman." His eyes were closed and he appeared to be kicked back and relaxed without a care in the world, even though he was being bounced around and his head bobbing at every turn. His smile had changed to one of climatic satisfaction.

On the day of graduation, the Apaches stopped me in the parking lot and asked me to come over to their vehicle. As they stood smiling, I was handed a cardboard box and told to open it. Sitting it down on the ground, I gingerly lifted the corners. Inside was a complete set of Apache Crown Dancers carved from cottonwood root; health, wealth, and prosperity and the fourth was to chase the evil spirits away. But wait, there was a fifth. For extra protection, I reasoned. It was hard to keep my mind on other things after seeing the beauty in that beat up old box.

The Navajo treated me to gifts as well leaving me overwhelmed with their generosity and thankful that the good Lord made me the way I was. I formed a bond with the Navajo and Apache officers from the first day of the academy; a bond that we all share to this day. There are no racial barriers, no language differences; just love, respect and admiration.

Shortly after graduation from the academy, Julie presented me with a new grand daughter. I held her in my arms for only a few short minutes, before I was already whispering Navajo in her precious little ear. Little Amanda was sweet and chubby with an ever-ready smile. She loved ice cream and French fries as a toddler. I always made sure she had French fries and my husband always made sure she had ice cream. That precious little creature, along with her little brother, Kenny became my life; and they still are. Both children say their prayers in Navajo every night; both receive an abundance of love and reciprocate it.

Julie merely smiles and says, "The tradition lives on."

Amanda used to be the practical one, wanting to save money and shy about having someone spend it on her. Kenny was just the opposite. He liked to feel the jingle of coins in his pocket and had a hard time holding on to it with all the temptations. Now as they grow older, their roles have reversed.

Over the years I've had many kids come and stay with me, both Anglo and Navajo. Many have been abused and come from homes where there wasn't enough love to go around. I've been there and understand, so my heart has always been open to these innocent children who did not ask to be brought into this sometimes cruel world.

Every time another child would enter my door, my mind would drift back to Chaco Canyon and I would find it hard to sleep that night. In Chaco, I vividly remember an old Navajo grandmother, with gnarled weaver's hands and tattered clothing, who approached me one moonlit night. She had two dirt encrusted little children in tow; a little boy and girl approximately 6 and 7 years old. Their matted hair was long and tangled in knots, their clothes tattered and worn; and oh God, their little faces were smudged with dirt. As they looked up at me with their pitiful little eyes, I could see how skinny and malnourished they were.

Grandmother explained that her daughter had left them with her and never returned. She was old and could no longer feed and care for them and wanted me to take them.

Why did she come to me? Probably because of the myth that since I was white, (and literally stood out in the crowd,) I was rich and could provide for them. If only poor Grandmother knew! The Navajo people were caring for me and feeding my children! Still, I entertained the thought of taking the children back to my hogan and caring for them.

I searched the crowd for Kee, to enlist his support. Together, we looked again for the grandmother. She and the two little ones had disappeared as quickly as they had come. Grandmother had probably found a ride home and couldn't wait for my answer; lest she and the little ones would be left with no ride home had my response been negative. I try to shut the picture of those innocent children and old grandmother out of my mind. But it doesn't work, even after all of these years. When I think of them, my heart weeps.

Living in a town where Indians would knock on my door at all times of the day or night definitely had some disadvantages, but at the same time, I got to know my people well. A couple of my "regulars" were two brothers who would show up inebriated, but I had a great respect for their mother, Sadie, and a comedy type relationship with her sons.

They were in their late twenties, of disheveled appearance and always in dire need of a bath. Still they made my day brighter with their antics and laughter. Once they needed money to buy a bottle of Thunderbird (cheap liquor) and having nothing to sell, resorted to digging through dumpsters. Knock, knock, knock came the sound at the front door. Rain was pouring down and I opened the door. The two brothers stood there grinning. One held a blanket that reeked of rancid garbage. I laughed at the sight of them, telling them they looked like two drowned rats with their stringy hair and rain running down their grimy faces. Of course I invited them in, instructing them to leave that disgusting blanket outside, not really sure if it was the blanket or them smelling so badly.

But the one brother clutched it tightly saying, "Oh, I can't leave this outside. It belongs to my mother."

"Why you little liar," I shouted. "Sadie didn't make that. You got that out of someone's dumpster!"

Suddenly, we all burst out laughing. They threw the blanket back out into the rain, and I fed them before they left.

One day I got a call from a federal undercover agent asking for my assistance on a case. After hearing it, I agreed to work with him. His instructions were to "dress down" and look like a street person. This agent, Loadberg, had worked with my husband as a patrolman before going to the Bureau of Indian Affairs, and also happened to be Navajo. He told me the day the sting was going down and gave me an approximate time he would pick me up. He arrived at the house and my husband was there to greet him. Acting like two schoolboys they laughed and reminisced about old times. When we were ready to leave, my husband sternly looked at Loadberg and said, "You better bring her back in the same condition she left in." Loadbergh promised but I wasn't the least bit worried. He would protect me with his life and I knew it.

My hair was straight, face void of makeup, jeans tattered and torn. Loady pulled over to an advantage point with full view as I exited the vehicle. I wore a body wire as precaution, and hopefully to pick up the bad guy's conversation. I had no sooner crossed the street than I spotted a group of Navajo. They saw me at the same time. In the group were the two brothers who had brought the rancid blanket to my door. Recognizing me, the group ran to me yelling, "Ya ta hey, Juddie!" They encircled me like the wagon train at dusk.

"Go away, guys. I can't talk right now." I broke the ranks, swearing under my breath and continued on. "Darn, I hope they didn't blow my cover," I whispered into the mike, as I glanced over my shoulder to their waves and shouts. I forgot to warn Loadberg I was familiar with a lot of these guys! I hope he isn't worried!

I aroused suspicion at one location I had been instructed to enter. I was leery of the bad guy, but thought I had pulled it off and left the building without a problem. I was to walk to a convenience market where Loadberg would pick me up, slowly making his way toward me, watching to see if I had been tailed. Thank goodness for backup! The bad guy sneaked out the door and was following me as I made my way to the rendezvous point. I glanced over my shoulder; saw him and my heart begin to pound. "Darn it Loadbergh! I hope you're close," I murmured under my breath. Even with the body wire I felt vulnerable, and stayed in highly visible areas, taking no short cuts. The bad guy continued to trail me without incident.

"Whew!" I gave a sigh of relief.

I was still concerned about my safety as I reached the convenience market, and I'll be, if it weren't the two brothers again. As I started to walk in the door they converged on me, this time without their friends.

"Come on, Juddie. Just give us $2 for a bottle of Thunderbird."

Juddie Cline-Lindley

"No way. Now get away from me" I said, still praying the bad guy wasn't close by. I was worried enough about my own safety. This was not a good time to worry about theirs as well. Besides, with the body wire every word was being recorded.

One of the brothers became a little miffed. Raising his hand limp wristed, he declared, "I hate you!" Then they ambled off to find a "new target" that might be intimidated into giving them money. I became amused thinking of federal agents listening to that tape! Unknowingly the brothers had put a bright spot in my day, and taken the jitters away.

A short time later a shaken Loadbergh picked me up, exclaiming he had pulled his gun when they surrounded me. All he could think of was my husband's explicit instructions; "You better bring her back in the same condition she left in." Loadbergh would have rather faced the bad guy if something had gone wrong.

I threw myself into police work, sometimes working over 75 hours a week. There was so much to learn and I wanted to "drink it all in" as quickly as possible. I was also interested in other work prospects and took a business trip to a mountainous community a few hours drive from our home. One look and I knew where I was. Many years before I had driven through there and saw the beautiful, flower-filled meadows and running streams. I had vowed then that someday, I would live there. That night I went home and told my husband it was time to move. He had retired from the Highway Patrol and had loved that area for many years himself, so it certainly didn't take any coaxing. We sold our home and purchased another one in our beautiful mountainous community.

We'd lived there just a few weeks when I had to run an errand several hours away. It was a February day and Little Amanda and Kenny were with me. My husband worked for the sheriff's office, and we were on our way to pick him up at work so he could go with us.

Kenny was a problem in a car. We nicknamed him "Houdini," because the little stinker could get out of any car seat. The longest it had ever taken was ten minutes, and every time we bought a new seat, we tried to convince ourselves that we had outsmarted him this time. Nothing seemed to work, so in making the forty-five minute drive to the sheriff's office, I always pulled over twice, to ensure he was strapped in securely. We never worried about Amanda. She was always obedient, generally listened to instructions, and complied the first time she was asked. Still, I would always ask, and always check her restraint as well as the little guy's at my regular stopping areas.

Both kids had nodded off shortly after the second security stop and we were on our way. Suddenly, a large piece of wood loomed in the middle of the narrow, two-lane highway. It had fallen off of someone's truck. I took evasive action, narrowly missing a culvert and the car began to whip and turn. We rolled down an area with such force that the vehicle landed on its roof and the front end took a nosedive, burying the car in the ground. Although I was belted in and it was a new car, somehow during the force of the roll, my body completely turned around and I was facing the back of my seat. I could hear both kids softly crying and to me that was a good sign; they were both alive. My end of the car was pitch black, like a tomb. I told myself out loud to stay calm and told Amanda the same. Then I said, "OK Jude, let's try step A." I undid my seat belt and immediately fell down backward into the steering wheel, having been suspended somewhat in mid air. Step B was to turn the motor off. Step C was to honk the horn. Step D was to kick the window out. I tried with no results, and screwed up my knee instead.

I continued to talk to Amanda, telling her to be brave and instructing her to undo her seat belt and release Kenny from his restraint. I told her if there was a way out, to take her brother to safety and I would join them shortly. She cried softly, but agreed to try.

Suddenly, I had a horrible feeling come over me. The baby was no longer crying. Oh God, was he dead? I managed to find a little crack and I could see through to the back seat. There was Amanda, covered in shattered glass and an older Navajo man on his knees at the back window. He was literally tearing the broken glass away with his bare hands. Then his hands went out to Amanda saying, "Come to me. Come to me."

She whimpered, "No, I'm scared."

I was able to reach through the crack and pick up a blanket with my fingertips, and hold it out to this man. Before leaving the house I had put the blanket in the car as an extra precaution for warmth in case of emergency. I instructed him to lay it across the broken glass and she would crawl out. He did so, and she crawled out so fast she reminded me of a scampering bunny rabbit.

I still could not see or hear the baby and feared the worst. Finally, I was able to free myself and quickly exited the vehicle. The police were there almost immediately. Several of them had just come from a training exercise and had been a short distance behind me. They quickly began to administer first aid to Amanda.

Still no baby.

One of the officers looked at me and said, "I know you."

I replied, "Yes, we just took a training class together a few weeks ago."

He had such a pained look in his eyes as I told him the baby was missing. Crawling on our stomachs, he took one side of the car and I took the other searching for the baby. We backed out, and re-entered on our stomachs, searching for Little Kenny. I crawled over a bump and a horrible feeling came over me. I began to shudder; almost feeling like I was lying on a grave. I looked at the other officer, shook my head, and we slowly backed out.

Dear God, how would I ever tell my husband our beloved baby was dead? Having exited the vehicle I was still on my knees, telling myself, "The baby's dead. Amanda's alive and I have to take care of the living." Suddenly a burst of sunlight came through the clouds as the wind was blowing hard. I was still on my knees as I looked up and saw a bright flash of color out of the corner of my eye. The wind had blown a Navajo lady's skirt so hard, that it was off to the side of her almost in a triangle. My eyes followed the color downward, and there was my beloved grandson standing at her feet.

An ambulance was dispatched for little Amanda. My husband and daughter had been notified and were on the way. The baby was thriving on the attention he was getting along with the stuffed bears given to him by the officers. Kenny never really liked being around females, and always responded to a male figure (too much time around grandpa!)

A vacationing couple stopped to help and offered to hold the baby, leaving me free to tend to Amanda. I thanked the lady but told her Kenny would feel more comfortable with her husband. Her husband smiled broadly and held out his arms; the baby responded by going into them without hesitation until the ambulance arrived.

At the hospital they determined that neither child had any injuries. Amanda was badly frightened but precautions had been taken at the scene. The investigating officer asked if I would like to have the name and address of the vacationing couple that stopped to help.

"Of course, but what about the Indians?"

The officer said, "What Indians?"

"The medicine man that pulled Amanda and the baby out," I replied.

The officer seemed puzzled and said that there were no Indians at the scene when he arrived, and he had been there within minutes of the call.

I knew I saw a Navajo medicine man help Amanda from the crumpled wreck. I could tell by the way he was dressed and his ceremonial jewelry. I also knew his wife had the baby at her feet protecting him from the wreckage. If this man had been Anglo, the children probably would not have gone to him. They have grown up with Navajo and I was sure that with all the turmoil they assumed the man was their Uncle Benny.

I have always taken great pride in the fact that I could locate just about any Navajo that I set out to find. But to this day, I have never found the Navajo man that helped care for the babies, and spare them from harm. I have looked high and low, contacting Navajo Chapter houses and spreading the word among the people. Still, he has never been found. Uncle Benny says I should stop looking and accept the fact that a Navajo angel spared the children. This was hard for me to accept at first. Now I find peace in it.

Navajo have traveled many miles to see the children. Acting almost reverently and serene, they sit and watch them play, never saying a word. They come to see this living miracle that a Navajo angel had a part in.

Election time was drawing near. The sheriff was running for re-election and having narrowly made it the last time, asked for my support in gaining the Native American vote. I had never been involved in politics and quite frankly, never wanted to be. But after careful consideration and viewing the candidates, I knew our current sheriff would be the best suitable candidate for the job and would treat the Indians in a fair and impartial manner. I talked with the sheriff and told him my requirements, advising him also that the medicine man would make the final decision.

First, the sheriff must have special prayers and go through a Blessing Way ceremony with Uncle Benny officiating, followed by an exchange of gifts. Second, there would be a feast and he had to supply the meat. Navajo would come to the gathering with lots of food, traditional dancing and prayers. It would be held outdoors with a big fire going and Navajo beating the drums. Was he willing?

"You bet," he answered.

"Good, the next time I talk with Uncle Benny a meeting will be arranged for you to meet in person. The final decision rests with my uncle. He'll read your heart."

In less than 48 hours Uncle Benny showed up on my doorstep. It was as though he already knew he was needed. I called the sheriff and he immediately left his office and came directly to my house. He met with Uncle Benny and the two talked about the Navajo people and safety measures and precautions that needed to be taken by the sheriff's office to protect the elders. They reached an amicable agreement, and Uncle Benny agreed to back the sheriff's election campaign with Navajo support. In short order, the word had filtered to the Navajo that Uncle Benny was supporting the sheriff. Navajo men and women began handing out campaign flyers, standing in the middle of dusty, old roads on the reservation to lend their support as well.

The sheriff supplied the beef for the ceremony, still on the hoof. Slaughtering went quickly. It was butchered, placed in burlap bags for baking and buried in the ground. The Blessing Way ceremony had to be done in a separate location away from the others. Prayers of this nature must be done by a medicine man under a tree that has been struck by lightning but yet lives. During the ceremony, three eagles circled overhead. Once it was completed we all returned to the prayer hogan at Uncle Benny's. There was an exchange of gifts, along with food and lots of fry bread and good conversation while a horny toad walked at our feet. A horny toad represents good things to Navajo and to have one appear at our feet, more or less sealed the deal.

As I was standing outside visiting, Mary, my Navajo sister, came to me whispering and acting very secretive. "Juddie, come with me, I need your help," she whispered.

Knowing this behavior was not normal for Mary, I asked if anything was wrong.

"Shuuu someone might hear you. I need your help." I followed Mary back into her humble house as she continued to glance over her shoulder to make sure we weren't being followed. She carefully lifted the handmade cotton curtain that covered the lower sink area and proceeded to drag a black plastic lawn and leaf bag out from under it.

"Juddie, come and help me. I don't want anyone to see."

I helped her drag the big bag to the middle of the room and she opened it so I could see her treasure. Inside were the head, eyes, hair and all from a slaughtered cow. Catching myself, so as not to laugh, I asked her what she was going to do with it.

"Why, make a stew this winter. I'll cook it outside."

"Mary, it still has hair on it. What are you going to do about that?" I asked.

"Leave it!" she replied.

"Well, I'm sure it'll taste good. Do you want me to help you hide it?"

The two of us drug the cow head to a new location and enlisted the support of a fellow police officer to help lift it, into a more secure hiding place.

The sheriff won the election. The Navajo felt they won too, for several reasons. Security for the elders was most important; and they had a feast they didn't have to pay for. Also, they proved to themselves; staying united, they had a voice.

I had been invited to attend a ceremonial dance at Uncle Benny's and I couldn't wait to attend. It was always thrilling and exciting to participate in the food and dancing. Late as usual, I stepped out of the car and could hear the prayers being sung and the drum beating. I felt a thrill, just like the very first time I had ever attended. Mutton stew was being served and hot fry bread was cooking over the open fire. I greeted the women, then asked where my uncle was, and learned he was in the prayer hogan saying prayers for the passing of the drum.

Jokingly, I said, "I can't believe he started without me. Please go tell my uncle I want to be in the prayer hogan."

I continued to eat and converse with people. Suddenly the drums stopped beating and the prayerful songs ceased. I figured the prayers must be over, not knowing how long they had been going on. Then a lady whispered in my ear. "Your uncle said it's all right to come into the prayer hogan."

I was floored! I had only been joking. But drums had stopped. The prayers had stopped. I better hurry and get in there!

Time passed and my husband died suddenly in the night. Suddenly, I was thrust into a surreal position of dealing with probate and relatives. I am not a weak person but I am a firm believer that God's time is not one to question, and there is a purpose for His actions. I also believe with all my heart, God looks after me, just like He did on the reservation. His love and protection will always be present and He will never leave or forsake me. God gives us life and there is an appointed time for it to be taken.

Juddie Cline-Lindley

CHAPTER 9

THE HEALING

I have spent most of my lifetime running away. Survival was always foremost on my mind. Saying goodbye to the Navajo people was so painful that I never wanted to relive that horrible heart wrenching pain again. I never wanted to get close to anyone, have close friends or live in one place too long. The joy and laughter I shared with my Navajo family would be embedded in my heart and soul, and a topic rarely discussed throughout my life. My love for them and the many secrets we shared would remain buried deep within. The anguish I felt over leaving my people tore at me as though there had been a death and a finalization. I knew I could not look back. I could not go back. Yes, there was happiness, the happiest years of my life. But there was also the pain: The mental and physical anguish at Bob's hands. The constant running and looking over my shoulder, seldom being able to relax and enjoy life to the fullest. And perhaps even guilt. Guilt for not being able to provide for my children in the way that I would have liked.

The Navajo people were there to rescue me in my time of need. They gave me purpose and being; teaching me the true essence of love and sharing; of having little but giving a lot. Living simply, but contently. Finding something to smile about even if it were a bird tugging away to pull a worm out of the ground, or watching as a Navajo crawled under a barb wire fence to reach the disputed land, or the laughter of small children as they played with a coyote puppy.

The day I said "goodbye" and left the reservation was without much fanfare. I never expected to see Kee or Albert and Suzie again. I always felt the pain and bitter memories of Bob would close the door behind me forever. I never wanted to look back. I wanted the bittersweet memories of the reservation along with the people I loved, to be locked in my heart. What little I shared of these memories was usually with my children. Occasionally I would let my guard down and say something around an Anglo and almost immediately the response would be a pitying, "Oh how could you have possibly have lived in a dirt floored hogan around Indians?" I soon learned people like that didn't merit an answer. I was the fortunate one. I had been blessed. I believe that materialistic people who ask that kind of question are probably still searching for some type of closure within themselves.

I don't consider myself a role model. I'm not a leader or a crusader. I strive daily to remain humble. Many people are searching for what I have embedded in my heart and soul. It's a simple word called peace. My journey has been different, more unusual than most, but through the years I've grown spiritually, mentally and physically. Had I not been embraced in love by the Navajo people, undoubtedly this "growth" and strength of convictions would never have blossomed into maturity. I like to have "material things" just like anyone else. Carpeting, air-conditioning, a comfortable home and car. But what we really need most is something I found almost 35 years ago on a desolate, wind swept Indian reservation in a remote area of New Mexico. I found a state of peace that many search for, and the love of a people who accepted me unconditionally.

I was thrust into a position with unusual circumstances. I had been battered, which we know is not that unusual. But I had no family to turn to and the strangers that did welcome me with open arms spoke a strange language unknown to me. They lived simply, many in dirt floored hogans or small tribal built homes with bare cement floors. They existed on a diet of mutton stew, fry bread and occasional cans of fruit. Their attire was such as I had never seen, and their expressionless faces lacked any visible signs of emotion. They were deeply committed to their beliefs, superstitious and without a shadow of a doubt, believed in dreams. These people called Navajo became my people; my family, and I reciprocated their love and respect by becoming extremely protective of them.

I carefully screen people that want to visit the reservation and meet my Navajo family members. I absolutely will not allow disrespect. I am the one held responsible for the actions of people that I take to meet my family. If they go with me, doors of hospitality and love await them; if they are discourteous, out of stupidity or ignorance, I will be the one that knocks on hogan doors apologizing for their behavior.

This is the unwritten rule, and one that I am in total agreement with. If you had a family member bring a guest home to meet your parents or siblings, and your family knew in advance of their coming and went to great time and expense to prepare a special meal, would it matter if it were steak or mutton stew? Would you be offended if your guest "turned up his nose" and declined to eat the prepared meal, even by politely saying, "No thanks, I'm not a meat eater, or I don't like mutton." Probably so, because you would take into account the feelings of your loved ones, along with time and money spent to please YOUR guest or friend. You would suffer embarrassment along with your family and that is not permissible, or something you can shrug your shoulders at and walk away from. It would have to be dealt with to everyone's satisfaction with the exception of the perpetrator. That category stands alone and there is no margin for error.

I always tell people when I do screening prior to taking them to the reservation; NEVER assume they don't speak English. Most of them either speak fluent English, or can understand enough words to know what the conversation is about. They may speak nothing but Navajo around a stranger, (after all it is their home) but only a very foolish person would assume they don't understand English.

The Navajo are very real, warm-hearted people. I like to call them, "what you see is what you get," type people. They don't put on pretentious airs. Why should they? Or why should any of us for that matter? Uncle Benny likes to study a person's eyes when he visits with them. He believes when he looks into their eyes, he can see their heart.

That's why he decided to support the sheriff in his re-election bid; and that's also why he allows me to partake in ceremonies and bring friends to his home. It is a child like love from the heart, with a pureness and simplicity without racial barriers. Is this an idyllic concept in an imperfect world?

I have learned many things from the Navajo over the years by watching, listening, questioning and finally embracing their teachings and beliefs. I give back to Mother Earth and listen to Father Sky. Isn't it all the same? Aren't we all seeking harmony and peace within? I don't disagree with the way Navajo believe any more than I do others. We're all striving for the same result; some have to go down different pathways to achieve this.

Recently my son became critically ill. Doctors advised the prognosis was dim. He was given less than a 1% chance of surviving the 30-minute flight to a major medical center. As I took short deep breaths to retain my composure, an ambulance was dispatched to take his unconscious life form to the small airport a short distance away. Upon arriving at the airport I noticed a mature cowboy looking individual who appeared to be waiting for us. As the ambulance doors opened and the plane made ready for boarding, the cowboy stood by, quietly observing, then gingerly approaching me, he carefully studied my face. He wore a cowboy hat and boots and from his mannerisms I quickly guessed he was a rancher that had lived in the area probably his entire life. His conversation began in soft-spoken tones, almost as though it were condolences.

"Is that your husband?" he asked.

"No, my son." I replied.

"Your son! You don't look that old."

"Why, I'm so old, I've got two feet in the grave," I half jokingly said.

The cowboy seemed surprised at my response and bantered me back, all the while searching my face for fear or hysteria over my son's lifeless appearing body. I knew I had to keep up a brave front. Now was not the time to become emotional; strength was essential. I could not give up. Just take one step at a time, I kept telling myself.

Suddenly the cowboy became quite somber and looking into my eyes spoke softly and said, "Is he going to make it?" Nodding his head toward my son.

"I don't know," was my firm reply.

Then this wonderful gentleman did something quite unexpected. The paramedics had pushed the gurney to the aircraft door. The cowboy moved swiftly over there, ordering them to stand aside. I remember how strangely they looked at one another, but immediately moved aside without speaking a word. Then the cowboy gently lifted the litter with my precious cargo and pushed it to the waiting personnel inside the craft. It was a simple but very personal gesture that left me feeling almost like being back on the farm again. In cases of death or tragedy, the neighbors and close friends would care for the family. There was never any room for "outsiders" or spectators. It was a time for caring and sense of loss shared by all. That's how I felt about this cowboy; this man who had been a complete stranger only a few minutes before. We were sharing as though we had known each other for years. He was caring for my son and wanted no one else to touch him.

Once in the air turbulence was throwing the small craft about. But I did not care. That was my son lying behind me. My thoughts trailed back before John was ever born. The doctor didn't give me much hope of carrying him and I spent a lot of time praying that God would make this baby a reality. I remember saying: "God this is your child, not mine. Just loan him to me, Lord." Now, years later, here I was in this aircraft transporting my critically ill son to a hospital. Instead of praying and begging God to save his life, I simply thanked God for allowing me to have him by my side for these years.

The medical team was waiting at the hospital. As the days passed he lay in an unconscious state, giving me a lot of time to think by his bedside. It became easy to remember the sights of the reservation, the smell of sizzling steak (bought or otherwise) over the open fire, and the aroma of coffee as it flitted through the air. I also remembered my reason for living there. I was looking at him in that hospital bed.

The Navajo had taught us to accept the simple way of life, living in harmony with nature one day at a time. To accept the passing of a loved one is difficult and painful for all of us. The Navajo are no exception. I have comforted a number of my Navajo who have been left with voids that only time can heal. Now, it may be my turn.

A Hopi friend of mine lost his little 9-year-old daughter to tragic circumstances. With broken heart and a flood of tears from us both, he talked of his devastation and pain. Oh, how he loved her and wished he could hold her in his arms! As time began to heal, he realized she had to leave him for just a little while. "Now, he said, I live one day at a time, knowing each day is just another day closer to being with her."

The experiences and love I and my children shared with the Navajo while living on the reservation blessed us and enriched our times. Those memories could never be taken away, and if it was time for my son's passing, I prayed for strength and acceptance knowing the Navajo people would be focused on me. We would bind together in love and our strength would sustain us.

"Dear God, if he must pass, please don't let me fail my people. Keep me strong for them," I prayed.

As strange as it may seem to some, Uncle Benny always knew when one of the kids were sick, and even if it were midnight, he'd show up at the door with his prayer bundle in his hand and ask, "Who needs me?" He lives in a remote area of the reservation with no phone service, and would travel for hours to reach us. I never had to call Chapter Houses or tribal police to get an emergency message to him. He just knew, and without fail, has always been there for me. My son's recent illness was no exception.

I was traveling back and forth daily from the medical center, only to find Uncle Benny waiting in the driveway the day after John had been admitted. I had no idea how long he had been sitting in his truck, nor do I think the hours would have mattered to him.

This dear man has never shown anger toward me; always love compassion and caring. But the instant I saw him, I could see signs of agitation on his face. The keys hadn't even been removed from the ignition before Uncle Benny had thrown open the truck door, lighting out toward me taking brisk steps.

"Where have you been! Who's sick? Who needs me?" he demanded.

"Uncle Benny, please come in and sit down. Here, let me get you some cool water," I offered as he entered the house. "Don't be angry with me. I wouldn't know how to deal with your anger, but today would be even worse." The tightness in his jaws seemed to relax and his anger appeared to subside as he slowly sipped on his glass of water and waited for my explanation without speaking.

Finally, drawing a deep breath, I began to tell him the critical situation. "It's John, Uncle Benny, he's very sick. The doctor doesn't think he will live." Uncle Benny's shoulders drooped low and a pained ashen look crossed his face. I could see he blamed himself for not coming sooner. Even this strong willed Navajo man could not hide his emotion or pain.

"It's OK Uncle Benny, John's still alive. Just say prayers for his recovery. You've done nothing wrong. You didn't fail me or let me down. I knew you would come." Uncle Benny insisted on saying prayers before he left that day, and clutching the eagle feathers tightly in his hand, prayed intently for my son. Vowing to see this through, Uncle Benny promised to return.

Several days had passed and my son, barely alive, still lay there with no apparent signs of improvement. That is, until his sister arrived. Then there was an immediate change in John. Throughout their childhood they constantly teased one another, and sibyl rivalry was rampant. Upon entering the room, Julie immediately went to John's bedside, and leaning over, whispered something in his ear. I don't know what she said, nor do I care. She stood there grinning as suddenly his fingers began to move, his eyelids flickered and he began moaning at what I perceived to be, an attempt at obscenities. My son was back! John was released after a miraculous recovery a few weeks later, but his journey of pain had just begun. There would be many hospitalizations in the future.

Uncle Benny made many subsequent trips to pray for John and check on his progress, insisting I practice my "prayers" or "songs" as the Navajo call them before he left. Ashamedly, sometimes I moaned out loud, over making a life time commitment. But Uncle Benny was relentless and insistent that I do the songs and chants with him before he left for the day. My progress is slow, over 40 years slow. Maybe someday, somehow, I will also know when I'm needed and unexpectedly show up on someone's doorstep regardless of the time or distance.

Life's journeys are sometimes strange and unpredictable; experiences are both good and bad. Some people refer to the negative as "bumps in the road." I like to think of the "bumps" as inconveniences that test our character and inner strength. That darn horse has bucked me off many times but a stubborn refusal to lay there and cry out, "I give up!" has seen me through some pretty tough times.

My son's refusal to give up and witnessing my brother's valiant fight against cancer has been an inspiration to me. I'm over-whelmed with pride knowing that both look (ed) upon their plight as an inconvenience with a refusal to allow death a win.

I've learned to speak up and say what I think and feel. Even retributions can be said with love and understanding. To put it bluntly, "Life's too short to do the two step." Say it, get done with it and continue on with your journey.

Uncle Benny began having lung problems, often touching his lung telling me there was pain. I would do prayers for him and burn cedar, pressing herbs in his hand before he left. My concern grew and I begged him to go to the Indian hospital for treatment. Reluctantly he complied and was almost immediately hospitalized for further testing.

The day of the biopsy the family gathered at the hospital and I, running late as usual came rushing in. Inquiring at the nurses' station the whereabouts of Benny Singer, I was sternly informed that only family members were allowed in with him. I didn't miss a beat! I told the nurse he was my dad and demanded to see him.

The nurse stammered a little and suggested there must be a mistake. The Benny Singer registered as a patient was a Navajo man.

I quickly replied that he was my adoptive father and insisted I be allowed to see him. I was ushered back by medical staff with quizzical expressions on their faces.

I found Benny lying on a bed in the hallway, waiting his turn for treatment while family members looked through the windows on the doors sporting wide grins. Finally, some of the kids slipped out and joined us, and laughed heartily as I told them of my experience gaining access. Benny laughed, too. Then becoming somber, he let his family know that I was his daughter, as well. From that day forth, I was to call him father.

The test results were negative; no tumors, no growths of any kind. Just too many years spent in smoke filled hogans praying for his people.

My son received word that Bob had died. I was in shock and disbelief. After all of these years, it must be another one of his horrible, sick tricks. Once it was confirmed, I called Julie.

"How do you know?"

"He's so evil, may, just maybe."

Julie said, "Mom he's dead. He can't ever hurt us again. I'm sure. He's dead."

I sucked in my breath and let it out slowly. I trembled and my body shook. After all of the years spent looking over my shoulder and sleeping with a gun under my pillow, or close enough to grab, the nightmare was finally over. No more sleepless nights and listening to every sound in the dark. It was finally over, and without a doubt, the gates of Hell were thrown wide open to welcome him.

The kids had jokingly called me a "vampire" for years. I could be sound asleep and jump out of bed at the least little sound. Because of him. Because of fear. But no more. I'm safe. My kids are safe. Because God took a monster from this world.

Over the years, healing had slowly taken place in my life and I hadn't even realized it. There are times I yearn for closeness and sometimes loneliness turns to longing, wishing to share. Maybe someday I will find a man with exceptionally strong inner strength. Perhaps he will be Navajo. Regardless, he will be mine and I will be totally devoted to him, and he to me. He will provide me with the strength I seek and be there for me in my dark hours; if not physically, then spiritually. I will know, for I will feel his presence and his prayers.

Will I find this mystery man? Imperfect, but yet perfect in my eyes? Only God knows. But I realize with all the time I spend at my son's bedside, hours stretch into days and days sometimes turn into weeks. There is no time to socialize or meet that special someone that makes me want to grab my heart and gives me butterflies in my stomach.

I spoke frankly with God late one night, blubbering and whining like a little sissy, burying my face in my pillow.

"Oh God," I said speaking softly and somewhat maturely. "I'm so lonely." In between sobs and sniffles I explained (and I thought I presented a pretty good case), what I really needed was a strong arm around my shoulders, whispering words of encouragement. "And God, the only way that is going to happen is if he walks in my door."

I felt better after the little talk with God that night. My strength was renewed and I look back and smile about our "special" talk. God could have struck me with lightning for speaking so boldly. Instead, I felt his warm smile and everlasting love.

The longing to return to Lake Valley in search of Kee Benally, Albert and Suzie seared my heart and soul, taking my sleep and leaving me restless. I argued with myself that returning after 35 years was inconceivable. But I was driven inside, searching for my roots so I could finally make peace with my past.

My stomach was tied in knots as areas began looking familiar and memories flooded me like a warm rain.

"This is the area where the witcher was, John herded sheep over there, I must watch out for the rattlesnakes this is a bad area." On and on I went reminiscing to myself. Finally, the long awaited tears began to pour. I was overcome with emotion and years of restraint could no longer hide them. I know the Great Spirit of the Navajo smiled warmly on me that day, making it permissible to cry and lay all strengths and weaknesses aside.

I didn't find Kee Benally that day, or Albert and Suzie; but what I did find was that same peace and love of people and land that was waiting for me with open arms almost 35 years ago. This time there were roads, even some pavement; electricity and water. My how things had changed! But something that would never change was the love and deep respect I have for the Navajo people, and I hoped that someday, when I found Kee, he would still feel the same about me.

A few months later, I went back to Lake Valley searching for Kee, or Albert and Suzie. I pulled over and parked and went knocking on hogan doors, clutching the one disintegrating picture of Kee that I had treasured almost 35 years. At one hogan I talked to a young Navajo man and woman who weren't sure if Kee was still alive, but said most assuredly that Albert and Suzie were and gave me directions to their home. The excitement began to rise and I tried to conceal my emotions and fight back the tears. My stomach was in knots. What if they didn't remember me? What if Bob had spread his web of deceit so convincingly, they didn't want me near them? What if, what if, "Lay it down, Jude," I told myself as I slowly worked my way up the bumpy road.

My heart felt like it was going to jump right out of my chest as I spotted Albert and Suzie's house. My God, give me strength! I got out of the car, and wanted to run to the door, but made careful deliberate steps. I knocked and a man answered. I studied him carefully and knew it was Albert! I tried to sound very professional as I told him I was looking for Kee Benally.

"Kee Benally?" he said, looking puzzled.

"Yes, I said, Kee Benally. I knew him many years ago. Here's his picture." I held up his picture and Albert held it in his hands, staring at it. Finally, I said, "Albert, look at me. Do you know me? Do you remember me? Can I come in and talk?"

Albert led me into his home, still with a puzzled look on his face.

Once again, I asked Albert if he recognized me. He looked deep into my eyes, and then suddenly sat down on the couch. His body slumped over. His shoulders and head hung low. He looked up at me with tears running down his face and said softly, "We were told you and the kids were dead."

We both cried over 35 years worth of tears as I reached for his hand to comfort him. "Oh, Suzie's not here today. She would want to see you," he kept repeating.

My heart kept crying out, "It doesn't matter, Albert. There will always be another day. I'll never leave you again." I couldn't get the words out, I was sobbing so loudly as we both sat and wiped away the floodgate of tears.

Albert was finally able to compose himself enough to tell me Kee had passed away about four years before. It was wintertime and he decided to drive his old truck somewhere. He got stuck. Like a typical Navajo, he got out and walked. He caught pneumonia from this and died a short time later.

All the uncertain years when my heart kept telling me to search for Kee, had finally come to an end. There will always be that void, that emptiness, and unspoken "thank you" that he deserved and I should have given him. And now it can never be said to him. Instead, I say it to his memory, his family and the Navajo people who loved us, accepted us and opened to us their hearts and their homes.

I often think of Kee and questions still fill my mind. Who *really* was Kee Benally? Now, I think I have the answer.

Kee was maybe what you'd call a complex person. He seldom showed expression and what little he did, he would immediately try to disguise it, usually by lowering his head with the dusty brim of his cowboy hat covering his face.

He was a "stone face" as are many Indians, lacking facial expression and outward emotions. Yet, his emotions did surface on occasion; anger, compassion, Christian love and caring.

Albert and Suzie Juan

Kee was used to hard times and what Anglos would consider a bitter way of life. But to him it was living. Leaving the reservation would have probably broken his spirit until he returned.

He was traditional but understood two cultures, Navajo as well as Anglo and was able to adapt and function to a degree with both, always preferring Navajo, of course.

His English was somewhat broken, but was to be admired for knowing and speaking both. He didn't use "proper English" and often used broken phrases or words ie: "Stay away from them Apaches, sis, them mean people." But he got his point across. To my knowledge, no one ever doubted or questioned him over his words or actions.

Kee served in the military and was very patriotic and proud of his service, and the exemplary example Navajo Code Talkers performed for their country. Still he downplayed his role, feeling that it was *his* privilege to have served his country.

He had a devilish sense of humor. Example: When driving down reservation roads, I would ask Kee which way to turn. He would laugh out loud and shout, "Ya ta hey to the right" or "Ya ta hey to the left," when I was within a few feet of my turn. Or if I was sitting in the back of a vehicle with the kids, he would turn and grin real big at the reservation dirt smudged across my face.

He was compassionate. When Julie was bit by the scorpion he knelt beside her, gently holding her hand praying in broken English.

When John wanted a dog, Kee found him a coyote puppy and carrying it in his arms presented him with it, a broad smile across his face as John buried his face in the fur.

Every time Grandmother and Grandfather had their food and blankets stolen by their nephew "because they were old and it was time to die," Kee would come get me to bring them fresh food and blankets.

Kee was a patient teacher. Never smiling or making fun of me as I "slaughtered" the Navajo language and slowly learned the customs and traditions of the Navajo. He patiently taught me about Mother Earth and Father Sky, the sacred mountains and secrets in the earth hidden by time.

He was giving and caring. Always making sure there was food in the cupboards and fresh water to drink; firewood in the winter and plenty of Blue Bird flour for fry bread.

Kee was kind to us, never asking anything in return or trying to impose his convictions or religious beliefs on me. If anything, he was probably surprised and amazed that I accepted him just the way he was without prejudice, which was commonplace at that time.

Kee was protective. In his heart he felt we were his charges and no doubt would protect us with his life, even if that meant "shooting his own people," often patting his front pocket to assure me his 25 auto was always with him. He protected me from the drunks and "took care" of the thieves stealing gasoline. They never returned or posed a threat again.

But there were two sides to Kee. The other was dark and menacing.

It would have been a grave mistake for anyone to lie to him. I don't think there would have been forgiveness. Kee was always forthright and honest, telling it like it was. Never trying to hurt, but knowing no other way than the simple plain truth.

Kee's reaction to the drunks that dared touch me, and the sickening thud of their bodies as they were thrown in the back of the pickup truck haunted me for years waking me from sound sleep.

The day the rattler tried to strike one of the kids and the sound of the crunch as Kee grabbed the shovel, slamming it down on the rattlesnake's head. Then, the hard deliberate steps he took as he threw it over the makeshift corral fence stating, "There, now the smell will drive the others away." And knowing full well he had broken tradition and a big taboo that day to save my child's life. (Navajo believe if you kill a rattler, some day a bigger, meaner one will come after you and find you.) Still he did not hesitate.

There was such anger and fury when he stomped the scorpion to death for biting Julie. Oh God, I often worried what he might do if another little kid would hurt her or John.

I watched his expression as he grabbed a rifle and searched for the skinwalker that was trying to witch me. I also watched his expression and nod of approval as necklace after necklace made of cedar beads was draped over my head to afford protection from the evil one.

Kee was traditional, believing in dreams and visions. Why else would he have taken us to his family and treated us with such respect? The Navajo people knew of our coming and a place was prepared with sheets on the bed and food in the cupboard (when all were scarce for them). We were accepted and loved because Kee Benally was instrumental in paving the way and opening the doors and hearts of the Navajo people.

Kee's expression and "grunt" made me know I learned correctly when placing the pottery shards back on the ground giving them back to Mother Earth.

Kee trusted me and my judgment. I was a good student how-a-bit stubborn and asking far too many questions, he tolerated me reminding me of my brother, Joe, from Boy's Town. Probably for this reason I was taken to see the dinosaur and privileged to learn so much.

Indeed, Kee Benally had two sides to him. As we say in law enforcement, he wore two hats. But this is what made Kee so interesting and intriguing. His demeanor was strong and forceful, yet quiet and gentle. He was stubborn, but secretly held a terrific sense of humor. He was resourceful. As a law enforcement officer I used to tell the Sheriff, "Just tell me what you want done. Don't ask me how I did it." That's how I felt about Kee. If there was a need, Kee saw that it was met. I didn't ask how.

Kee Benally was my friend. He was my protector. He was my teacher, guiding me with patience and love. I, on the other hand, tried to be a good pupil and have benefited from it greatly over the years. Kee was my confidant and someone I trusted with my life and the lives of my children.

Kee opened the doors of the Navajo Reservation and gave my life meaning and purpose. He taught me about courage, love and giving of one's self. Taking one day at a time and walking in beauty as taught in Navajo way. He filled my heart and soul with riches beyond measure. He was my benefactor and taught me things that money can't buy. When I think of you, Kee, I want you to be proud of me as well as yourself. You did good, my friend. I shall never forget you.

Juddie Cline-Lindley

JUDDIE CLINE-LINDLEY

has walked among the Navajo for many years, having gained their love and respect. She and her children have always considered it a privilege to live on the Navajo Reservation, sharing rich experiences and the love of a people who have given much and asked little in return.

navajolittlesister@yahoo.com